Youn[g]

2004 POETRY

# ONCE UPON A RHYME

IMAGINATION FOR
A NEW GENERATION

## Poems From
## The East Of England
Edited by Steph Park-Pirie

First published in Great Britain in 2005 by:
Young Writers
Remus House
Coltsfoot Drive
Peterborough
PE2 9JX
Telephone: 01733 890066
Website: www.youngwriters.co.uk

SB ISBN 1 84460 687 2

# Foreword

Young Writers was established in 1991 and has been passionately devoted to the promotion of reading and writing in children and young adults ever since. The quest continues today. Young Writers remains as committed to engendering the fostering of burgeoning poetic and literary talent as ever.

This year's Young Writers competition has proven as vibrant and dynamic as ever and we are delighted to present a showcase of the best poetry from across the UK. Each poem has been carefully selected from a wealth of *Once Upon A Rhyme* entries before ultimately being published in this, our twelfth primary school poetry series.

Once again, we have been supremely impressed by the overall high quality of the entries we have received. The imagination, energy and creativity which has gone into each young writer's entry made choosing the best poems a challenging and often difficult but ultimately hugely rewarding task - the general high standard of the work submitted amply vindicating this opportunity to bring their poetry to a larger appreciative audience.

We sincerely hope you are pleased with our final selection and that you will enjoy *Once Upon A Rhyme Poems From The East Of England* for many years to come.

# Contents

| | |
|---|---|
| Andrew Lawrence (10) | 46 |
| Sophie Bannis (10) | 46 |
| Harriet Greenhill (10) | 47 |
| Russell Meddings (11) | 47 |
| Joshua Steer (10) | 47 |
| Emma Isbell (10) | 48 |
| Edwad Guest (10) | 48 |
| Chloë Herring (11) | 48 |
| Elizabeth Portsmouth (10) | 49 |
| Naomi Babalola (10) | 49 |
| Emily Higgs (10) | 50 |
| Claire Tibbott (10) | 50 |
| Lois Holmes (10) | 50 |
| Leanne Walker (10) | 51 |
| Charlotte Ross (10) | 51 |
| Rachel Vallance (11) | 51 |
| Melanie Marsden (10) | 52 |
| Kayleigh Gibbs (10) | 52 |
| Jonathan Sheppard (10) | 53 |
| Paris Parnell (10) | 53 |
| Jonathan Neale (10) | 54 |
| Peter Sheppard (10) | 54 |
| Lucy Waine (10) | 55 |
| Kirsty Chesney (10) | 55 |
| Tosin Olagundoye (11) | 56 |
| Paige Blackman (10) | 56 |
| Amy Austin (10) | 57 |
| Bonnie Rayner (10) | 57 |
| Paige Slade (10) | 57 |
| Joanna Rainbird (10) | 58 |
| Bryony Clark (10) | 58 |
| Victoria Walsh (10) | 59 |
| Katie Walker (10) | 59 |
| Mitchell John (10) | 59 |
| Joshua Daly (10) | 60 |
| Faye Freeman (10) | 60 |
| Marie Hawkins (10) | 60 |
| Jay Haxell (10) | 61 |
| Rachel Jones (10) | 61 |
| Robert Lord (10) | 62 |
| Eden Pickton (11) | 62 |
| John Coombes (10) | 63 |

| | |
|---|---|
| Jessica Chesney  (7) | 82 |
| Jake Farmer  (7) | 82 |
| Folasade Cline-Thomas  (7) | 82 |
| Elizabeth Hawkins  (7) | 82 |
| Holly Peck  (7) | 83 |
| Temi Abatan  (8) | 83 |
| Charlie Turner  (7) | 83 |
| Hannah Lauder  (10) | 84 |
| Lynden Reed  (7) | 84 |
| Beth Lamb  (7) | 84 |
| Aiden Jackson  (8) | 85 |
| Alexandra Wilding  (7) | 85 |
| Sian Smith  (7) | 85 |
| Abigail Morgan  (8) | 86 |
| Megan Togwell  (7) | 86 |
| Ashleigh Doman  (7) | 86 |
| Thomas Steer  (7) | 87 |
| Naomi Barwick  (8) | 87 |
| Hannah Sayers  (7) | 87 |
| Rachel Phelan  (7) | 88 |
| Madeleine Weekes  (7) | 88 |
| Luke Sheridan  (7) | 88 |
| Nathan Jackson  (8) | 89 |
| Oliver Portway  (7) | 89 |
| Harry Bradford  (7) | 89 |
| Nathan Smith  (8) | 90 |
| Naomi Vallance  (7) | 90 |
| Charlotte Neale  (7) | 90 |
| Victoria Christmas  (7) | 91 |
| Hannah King  (8) | 91 |
| Karen Morris  (7) | 91 |
| Jade Hill  (8) | 92 |
| Rosie Webber  (7) | 92 |
| Samuel Gowland  (7) | 92 |
| Fraser Clark  (7) | 93 |
| Chloe Hammond  (7) | 93 |
| Elizabeth McDonald  (9) | 93 |
| Ebenezer Oluwole  (9) | 94 |
| Sophie Doyle  (9) | 94 |
| Ryan McNamara | 94 |
| Daisy Harper  (9) | 95 |
| Albert Parnell  (9) | 95 |

| | |
|---|---:|
| Michael Stannard  (9) | 95 |
| Emma Cottrell  (9) | 96 |
| Abigail Howson  (9) | 96 |
| Jaron Escoffery  (8) | 96 |
| Rachel Stewart  (9) | 97 |
| Rianna Veares  (9) | 97 |
| Rowanne Simpson  (9) | 97 |
| Antony Dashfield  (9) | 98 |
| Deanna Newstead | 98 |
| Samuel Cockburn  (8) | 98 |
| Daniella Anderson  (8) | 99 |
| Olajoke Olaniyan  (8) | 99 |
| Alice Pugh  (8) | 99 |
| Max Lagrossi  (8) | 100 |
| Sophie Hughes  (8) | 100 |
| Emma Hatwell  (8) | 101 |
| Claire Jackson  (9) | 101 |
| Misha Goddard  (8) | 102 |
| Sarah Brown  (8) | 102 |
| Rachel Podd  (8) | 102 |
| Sophie Bowtell  (8) | 103 |
| Raelle Pickton  (8) | 103 |
| Élise Herring  (9) | 103 |
| Jack Hull  (8) | 104 |
| Abbie Legallienne  (8) | 104 |
| Jessica Stone  (9) | 105 |
| Emma Aston  (8) | 105 |
| Gemma Willson  (8) | 105 |
| Imogen Rayment-Smith  (8) | 106 |
| Sam Blowers  (9) | 106 |
| Alexander Hardy  (8) | 106 |
| Christian Wroe  (7) | 107 |
| Jessica Pitts  (8) | 107 |
| Elena Sheridan  (8) | 107 |
| Katherine Miller  (8) | 108 |
| Libby Ryder  (8) | 108 |
| Michael Nance  (8) | 108 |
| Joel Oyelese  (8) | 109 |
| William Borg  (8) | 109 |
| Jake Gear  (8) | 109 |
| Siân West  (8) | 110 |
| Pollyanna Clark  (9) | 110 |

Harlie Cornish  (10)                                          128
Rosie Ranson  (9)                                            129


## South Wootton Junior School, King's Lynn
Bethany Smith  (8)                                           130
Scarlett Fountain  (8)                                       130
Kasey Cannon  (8)                                            131
Holly Young  (8)                                             131
Madeleine Massingham  (8)                                    132
Jonathan Harvey  (11)                                        132
Georgeina Jarman  (8)                                        133
James Cave  (10)                                             133
Daniel Cummings  (8)                                         134
Jessica Morgan  (8)                                          134
Emily Ballard  (8)                                           135
Nadine McCrory  (8)                                          135
Freya Le Serve  (10)                                         136
Mark Britton  (8)                                            136
Adnaan Tyabjl  (9)                                           137
Ellen Walker  (8)                                            137
Vishaal Thakrar  (8)                                         138
Michael Playford  (8)                                        138
Ben Creevy  (9)                                              139
Joseph McLauchlan  (8)                                       139
Brandon Catterall  (8)                                       140
Marcelle McDonald-Leslie  (8)                                140
Sam Miller  (10)                                             141
Arrianne Gagen  (9)                                          142
Georgia Freeman  (10)                                        142
Zane Lin Tham  (8)                                           143
Matthew Hayward  (10)                                        143
Natalie Panks  (10)                                          144
Francesca Jarman  (10)                                       145
Evalyn Drake  (8)                                            146
Carys Gill  (8)                                              146
Kate Dewey  (11)                                             147

# The Poems

# Moths In The Bathroom

If there were three
there'd be a home for thee.

If there were four
there'd be a lot more.

If there were five
there'd be a nest or hive . . .
and a bee going whee!

If there were six
now let's get this fixed.

If there were seven
I'd go to Heaven.

If there were eight
let's get this straight.

If there were nine
they wouldn't be mine.

If there were ten
there's a home for them then.

But if there were eleven
I'd go straight to seven.

**Bobbi Talbot (6)**


# My Nan Jess

She sleeps like a cat
And forgets to take off her hat
She laughs, she's like a bird
And I can't believe that next door heard
Her hair is like a cloud
And she is so loud.

**Rachel Lynch (8)**
**Admiral's Junior School, Thetford**

# Custard

It's creamy and delicious, and only for me,
It's what I'm having for my tea,
It tastes so scrummy,
So yellow and yummy,
It's better than mustard
As it's good old *custard!*

**Kerry Douthwaite  (8)**
**Admiral's Junior School, Thetford**


# Gorilla

There he sits big and hairy
Strong as an ox and very scary
If you put your fingers in his cage
You could send him into a rage
All the signs say *Keep Away*
I think I will because this hairy monster wants to play.

**Tayler Dunkley  (8)**
**Admiral's Junior School, Thetford**


# Snakes

Snakes slither silently through the glorious green grass
Hissing steadily as they try to pass
Their skin so rough, like a crinkled paper bag
Tongues like forks poking in and out
I wish I could have one of them.

**Joshua Chamberlain  (8)**
**Admiral's Junior School, Thetford**

# Books

Books occupy me
Books are fun
Books are everywhere, even in a plum
They're fun, fun, fun!
They make my brain expand
Like a rubber band
I wonder why they call them bookworm
That's why I'm concerned
That's enough of books today
I hope next time I pick up a book it's not May
That's along way away.

**Louise Everist  (8)**
**Admiral's Junior School, Thetford**


# Cats

I love cats,
They're cute and cuddly,
Soft and fluffy,
And very, very quiet.
Climb steep trees,
Friendly and very lovely.
Some are thin, some are fat.
Sleep all day and hunt all night.
They lick themselves to get clean,
They curl up with their long tail.

**Bethany Rundle  (8)**
**Admiral's Junior School, Thetford**

# Remember!

Remember when the world was small
And you were tall
Paul's legs were all very tall
Thin legs, fat legs, dog legs and cat legs
Table legs, chair legs, dark legs, fair legs, your legs
Jumping legs, prancing legs, skipping legs, dancing legs,
        That's everyone's legs.

**Jessica Chapman (8)**
**Admiral's Junior School, Thetford**


# Windy Days

Sometimes wind is rather nice,
Other times wind is cold as ice.
Wind, wind, i like you a lot,
I like you better when it's hot.

**Victoria Scott (8)**
**Admiral's Junior School, Thetford**


# Dolphins Are Blue

Dolphins are blue
Dolphins all shiny and blue
They jump over sea
And dive back in
They're wonderful creatures
I tell you they are
Dolphins are blue.

**Alyssa Bursell (8)**
**Admiral's Junior School, Thetford**

# Cheeky The Monkey

Cheeky is a monkey
Cheeky as can be
She likes to go out shopping
And sometimes she takes me.

She likes all the clothes shops
As far as I can tell
She also likes to keep in fashion
Because she dresses really well.

When we have finished
And when the day is done
We go home very happy
Because the day was full of fun.

**Armarnie Senior  (8)**
**Admiral's Junior School, Thetford**


# My Mum

My mum is precious,
My mum is sweet,
My mum has the birthday beat,
My mum eats bananas in her pyjamas,
I love my mum because she's fun.

**Jake O'Connor  (8)**
**Admiral's Junior School, Thetford**


# Custard Is Yellow

Custard is yellow like mustard,
Custard is yellow like the sun,
Custard is warm and creamy,
And yummy in my tum.

**Elise Daw  (8)**
**Admiral's Junior School, Thetford**

# My Teacher

*My teacher is the best of all*
She has pretty white hair
That blows in the wind
She helps everyone and especially me.

*My helper:*
My helper is the best of all,
And he helps everywhere in my school.
He helps everyone in my class,
And especially me.
That person will be Mr Wake.

**Ellen Field  (8)**
Admiral's Junior School, Thetford

# Snakes

Three slimy, naughty snakes
slithered to a shop
and stole some cakes.

They slithered to the park
and ate them all up.

Now the three slimy snakes
have all got tummy aches.

**Rebecca Dixon  (8)**
Admiral's Junior School, Thetford

# Big Fat Gorillas

Big fat gorillas lying on their back,
All the ones I've seen are very fat.
Lying in the sun eating bananas,
Also putting on their pyjamas.
They like to rumble in the jungle,
And eat apple crumble.

**Sam Coleman  (8)**
Admiral's Junior School, Thetford

# Homer Simpson

Homer Simpson is lazy and fat,
He can't stop eating, fancy that.
He likes to eat doughnuts and pork chops,
He drinks Squishee at the local shop.
He works for Mr Burns, he is a millionaire,
Mr Burns is old and barely has any hair.
Bart, Lisa, Maggie and Marge,
Are his family, but he is in charge.
He lives in Springfield Town, a very nice town at that,
Homer has a dog and he also has a cat.
Homer is very funny, he makes me laugh,
He likes to sing when he is in the bath.
You might know him for shouting, 'D'oh!'
If he wants to drink Moe's is where he will go.
Homer is the best, a really cool man,
I like him very much and I am his biggest fan.

**Ayden Wheeler  (8)**
**Admiral's Junior School, Thetford**


# Spring

Spring is a lovely time of the year,
All the people come out and cheer.
All the flowers seem to pop out and appear,
The trees are full of blossom and smell so sweet.

The birds come out and sing in spring,
It's such a lovely time of year
For the birds to come out and sing in spring.
The air smells so fresh and seems to be so clear in spring.

**Zoe Samwell  (8)**
**Admiral's Junior School, Thetford**

# Cats

Cats, cats, they are so sweet
And they curl around your feet.

Cats, cats, they are so funny
They like it when you rub their tummies.

Cats, cats, they are so furry,
But they are also very purry.

**Ruby Adams (8)**
Admiral's Junior School, Thetford

# I Had A Pet Cat

*(In loving memory of my pet Razzy,
aged 20 years 8 months)*

My cat was black, as black as can be,
I loved my cat and my cat loved me.

He used to play with a piece of string,
And when he purred he used to sing,
I loved my cat and my cat loved me.

His whiskers were white and his fur was black,
When I stroked him he'd lift his back,
I loved my cat and he loved me.

He was old and going grey,
So very tired he'd sleep all day,
I loved my cat and he loved me.

We took him to the vet, the vet put him down,
Then we buried him under the ground,
I loved my cat and my cat loved me.

He's in Heaven now, the brightest star,
Looking down on me from very far,
I loved my cat and he loved me.

**Jemma Holmes (9)**
Admiral's Junior School, Thetford

# Farm Life

Down on the farm,
The pigs go oink, oink.

Down on the farm,
The hens go cluck, cluck.

Down on the farm,
The horses go neigh, neigh.

Down on the farm,
The dogs go woof, woof.

Down on the farm,
The birds go cheep, cheep.

Down on the farm,
The mice and rats run through the grass.

Down on the farm,
The rabbit goes hop, hop.

Down on the farm,
The life goes on . . .

**Alan Salter  (8)**
**Admiral's Junior School, Thetford**


# The Fox

I dreamt I saw a fox,
It had a golden chest;
A sly face looked back at me,
Its dark black nose sniffed the leafy ground.

Its beady eyes looked round gazing through the woods -
Then he raced off and that was the last I saw of him.

**Emma Smith  (9)**
**Blackmore Primary School, Blackmore**

# The Badger

I had come back from the park,
It was very, very dark.
The badger sat there in the light,
Beady eyes alight.
It was there, it was there,
I know it is rude but I had to stare.
While I stood there unable to move,
Its hair stood on end all soft and smooth.

This creature was there,
I wanted to move but I didn't dare.
I saw the badger's trembling ears,
It looked as if it had many fears.
It was there, it was there,
A dog barked but it didn't care.
Then it went back into its sett,
I didn't want to leave it yet.

**Jessica Morse (9)**
**Blackmore Primary School, Blackmore**


# When I Saw A Dolphin

When I saw a dolphin,
It jumped straight out of the deep, dark water.
Its long, sleek body
Shimmering in the moonlight like the sky's blue.

I watched it from the old, wooden jetty,
Diving through the deep, dark water.
It leapt so high,
It dived so low,
Oh I'll never forget that night.

**Emily Dimond (8)**
**Blackmore Primary School, Blackmore**

# The Golden Retriever

Yesterday I saw a golden retriever
Walking towards a dark, gloomy wood,
She had smooth, light golden fur
With a pointy, shaggy tail.

She had a tiny black nose
Just like a button,
She had short, soft ears
Like a teddy bear.

She had brown, glittering eyes
Just like gold,
It was so playful and cuddly,
I wish I had that puppy.

**Annabel Cakebread  (9)**
**Blackmore Primary School, Blackmore**


# My Puppy

I came home,
I saw my puppy,
She was so excited,
With golden fur and her black button nose,
And twitchy whiskers so fine.

Then I saw her run, run, run,
Down the massive garden of green,
The big, bold sun reflecting
On the pup's fur of gold.

**Jade Clifford  (9)**
**Blackmore Primary School, Blackmore**

# I Dreamt I Saw A Fox

I dreamt I saw a fox
As orange as the sun,
Jumping and·pouncing through the air
With its bushy tail.

I dreamt I saw a fox
With its nose as black as coal,
Clambering about like a hungry predator,
Ready to catch its prey.

I dreamt I saw a fox
Its sly eyes all brown,
It sniffed the ground with its huge snout
Then scurried down a dusty hole.

**Robyn Evans  (8)**
**Blackmore Primary School, Blackmore**


# I Dreamt I Saw A Fox

I dreamt I saw a fox last night,
Ginger with pointy ears,
He stood out in the dark forest,
Because of his beady eyes.

He was proud, but sly,
And pranced about,
He swished his tail,
And pounced into the deep green grass.

**Abbie Whitmore  (9)**
**Blackmore Primary School, Blackmore**

# Once I Saw A Unicorn

Once upon a dream,
I went for a walk at night,
I saw a sparkling light,
I thought it was a stray moonbeam,
Until I realised what it really was . . .

A beautiful unicorn,
Galloping happily through the dark forest,
Its silver horn, its beady eyes so alight,
Its breathtaking mane, its glittering hooves,
The unicorn was the most wonderful I had ever seen.

It pawed the cold midnight air,
And snorted a friendly snort,
The shining white unicorn proudly tossed its head,
And cantered off into the mossy space between the trees.

**Siân Juniper (9)**
**Blackmore Primary School, Blackmore**


# The Penguin

I dreamt I saw a penguin,
At my bedroom door,
It waddled straight at me.

It had a golden breast as yellow as the sun,
Its feet were as black as the night,
As it went into the light.

Its stomach white as snow,
Its beak as pointy as a pin,
I'll never forget that penguin.

**Samuel James (9)**
**Blackmore Primary School, Blackmore**

# Penguin

I dreamt I saw a penguin
Gliding on the ice,
They really are quite nice.

I dreamt I saw a penguin
With its bulging, golden chest,
They really are the best.

I dreamt I saw a penguin
As golden as the sun,
They look like lots of fun.

I dreamt I saw a penguin
Its head as black as night,
Then it waddled out of sight.

**Ieuan Lister (9)**
**Blackmore Primary School, Blackmore**


# The Day I Saw A Puppy

I saw a puppy,
One day in the park,
I said, 'Do you hear me?'
I saw a puppy near me.

I stroked it firmly,
His shiny, wet, black nose sniffed me,
He started jumping and bouncing,
And gave me a sloppy kiss.

**Rianna Perry (8)**
**Blackmore Primary School, Blackmore**

# My Dream

I dreamt I saw a horse last night,
It flicked its golden mane,
It jumped and neighed in the middle of the night,
It swished its silky tail,
It stood silently,
I made my way closer,
It suddenly disappeared off into the wood.

**Milly Moore (8)**
Blackmore Primary School, Blackmore


# One Day I Saw A Rabbit

One day I saw a rabbit,
With silky, golden fur,
He leapt out of his deep, dark burrow,
And twitched his tiny nose.

His beautiful beady eyes,
His droopy lopsided ears,
His white bushy tail,
Vanished into thin air.

**Rachel Whalley (8)**
Blackmore Primary School, Blackmore


# I Saw A Fox

I saw a wild fox yesterday,
It had pointy ears and golden fur,
It raced out from its dirty den,
And hunted for a meal.

The fox silently moved around,
It searched and searched and then found its prey,
It sprinted back as fast as it could,
And dived back into its den.

**Amy Warwick (9)**
Blackmore Primary School, Blackmore

# Seasons

Spring is for blossom
and spring is for trees,
Spring is for happy times
and spring is for bees.

Summer is for ice creams
and summer is for fun,
Summer is for playing games
and summer is for sun.

Autumn is for hedgehogs
and conkers in the trees,
Autumn is for chilly nights
and the cooling breeze.

Winter is for snowmen
and winter is for jellies,
Winter is for eating pies
and winter is for wellies.

**Sophie Fulker (10)**
**Chalkwell Hall Junior School, Leigh-on-Sea**


# The China Man

Ching chang China man
Had a pretty dog
He washed and dressed it
And called it Pretty Pol
He sent for a doctor
But the doctor wouldn't come
Because he had a pimple on his
Bum, bum, bum.

**Miles Harvey (8)**
**Chalkwell Hall Junior School, Leigh-on-Sea**

# Flying

If I could fly imagine what it would be like,
Flying above the clouds and the sea,
Flying above the school, think how small it would be,
If I could fly to school, I wouldn't be stuck in a car,
Getting all hot and sweaty,
If I could fly it would be like a bird flying to a tree,
Flying, flying away.

**Rebecca Marriott (9)**
**Chalkwell Hall Junior School, Leigh-on-Sea**


# The Big Black Belly

The Big Black Belly
Is really, really smelly
He comes out at night
And always wants a fight.

He never gets paid
And he hides in the shade
He never gets seen
And is really, really mean.

He calls himself Big Foot
Because his feet are so green and huge
He doesn't like his manners
He only likes his food.

He lives in a bin
And eats human skin
He hates the colour pink
And he really, really stinks
And of course, he never ever thinks.

**Darius Horban (9)**
**Chalkwell Hall Junior School, Leigh-on-Sea**

# Senses Poem

I like to watch . . .
Scary movies on Virgin Airways' aeroplanes,
Butterflies flutter by,
The calm sea ready to splash.

I like to listen to . . .
The deep warmth of my dad's voice,
The birds singing a sweet song,
The low notes of my saxophone.

I like to smell . . .
The lovely drifting smell of Pizza Hut making me want more,
The sweet scent of flowers,
Mincemeat drifting up my nose.

**Sophia Latif (8)**
**Chalkwell Hall Junior School, Leigh-on-Sea**


# Conkers

Everybody is going bonkers for conkers
Things are flying in the air
Conkers falling everywhere
Shaking branches off the tree
One for you and one for me
People climbing up the trees
Shaking down all the leaves
Spiky shells on the ground
I can see them all around
Fighting, pushing in a brawl
Crawling, grappling on the floor
Shouting, screaming, 'This one's mine
Oops! We are nearly out of time.'
'There's a conker or is it a shell?
We have to go now it's the bell.'

**Paige Adams (9)**
**Chalkwell Hall Junior School, Leigh-on-Sea**

# AC Milan Barbecue

My mummy is a sailor
My daddy is some ham
He got cooked on the barbecue
By the team AC Milan.

**James Marshall  (8)**
**Chalkwell Hall Junior School, Leigh-on-Sea**


## Fred's Ants

Once there was an elephant called Fred,
Who slept in a cardboard bed.
He had very big pants, which were full of ants,
And Fred said, 'These ants are taking a chance!
Last night I had a curry and if they don't hurry,
They'll end up worse than dead.'

**Osten Burrows  (8)**
**Cringleford CE First & Middle School, Norwich**


# Homework

I hate to do homework on Saturday,
It makes me feel quite sick,
I'd rather go outside and play,
I would take an ice cream to lick.

I hate to do homework on Sundays as well,
It makes me feel quite queasy,
If I have to do homework I will start to yell,
Unless it is easy peasy.

**Emily Hoogkamer  (8)**
**Cringleford CE First & Middle School, Norwich**

# The Man Who Fell In Love With A Plant

I know this sounds unusual
But a man fell in love with a sunflower.
He watered it every day and kissed it every night.
But all his friends thought he was mad,
So they took him to a mental surgeon,
But he just said, 'Well, well, never in my life
Have I come across a dude who fell in love with a sunflower,
I really can't believe you!'
'Oh, oh,' he cried, 'do believe us so!'
But they didn't.
So the man just kept on loving the sunflower for the rest of his life.

**Louis Narayn  (8)**
**Cringleford CE First & Middle School, Norwich**


# The Train

The train is an elephant
charging up the track.
Tooting his trunk at the station,
off-loading heavy loads from his grey back.

The train is an elephant
sneezing steam out of his trunk.
Stamping his feet on the rails
with an unck, unck, unck.

The train is an elephant
leading the herd.
Carriage to carriage, nose to tail,
over hill and down the dale.

**Sam Doyle  (8)**
**Cringleford CE First & Middle School, Norwich**

# My Granny's Dogs

My granny's dogs
Slobber everywhere
On my sister
In my hair
On the table
On the chair
On the bench
In the park
Slobber, slobber
After dark

On my bed
That is pink
On the dishes
In the sink
On the floor
On the walls
Even in the kitchen drawers
Yucky slobber
All the time
I still love them
Because they're mine.

**Lily Evans  (8)**
**Cringleford CE First & Middle School, Norwich**

# Silvery Snow

Softly, quietly silvery snow,
Reaches for the ground below.
She peers around the silvery floor,
And at the other snowflakes hanging on the door.

As she leapt from the heavens above,
She flew to the ground like a dove.
As the others fall and glide,
She observes the snowflakes at her side.

**Charlotte Hunting  (10)**
**Engayne Primary School, Upminster**

# Mighty Man

I have a dad named Bill
Whose head is as big as a seal
His hair is black and spiky
And he looks strong and mighty
His eyes are very dark and red
Like he woke early out of bed
His nose is as hairy as a monkey
His teeth are very chunky
His chin is as fat as an elephant
And he always acts like a pelican
His ears are as big as a giraffe
And he always has a laugh.

**Sam O'Dowd  (8)**
**Engayne Primary School, Upminster**


# Scribble, Scrabble, Bubble, Bang

*Scribble, scrabble, bubble, bang*
The lapping ocean sang
*Scitter, scatter, rumble, rum*
Shouted the mice on the run
Tilting and slanting
The boat rumbled on
*Scribble, scrabble, bubble, bang*
*Scitter, scatter, rumble, rum*
The squeak of the mice
Hear the big waves come!

**Scott Laverick  (8)**
**Engayne Primary School, Upminster**

# What Do Babies Do?

Mum, what do babies do?
They feed and sleep and cuddle too
Then they grow up to be like you.

Dad, what do babies do?
They laugh and cry and they learn to chew
Then they grow up to be like you.

Brother, what do babies do?
They scream and shout and wee and poo
Then they grow up to be like you.

Sister, what do babies do?
The learn to talk, walk and use the loo
Then they grow up to be like you.

So babies sleep and cry and scream and wee
Then they grow up to be like me.

**Jodie Edwards (9)**
**Engayne Primary School, Upminster**

# The Stream

Softly, steadily, now the stream
Stumbles the night in her pleasant dream.
Forward and back she stares and sees
Dancing buds upon dancing trees.
One by one her droplets fly
Merrily up into the sky.
Her water wades over a log
Lighting up the darkened fog.
The water takes a gentle stroll
Bumping up the water rolls.

**Sophie Mould (10)**
**Engayne Primary School, Upminster**

# Alone On An Island

Alone on an island,
Except the things I see.
Crabs wobbling on the sand,
Fish swimming in the sea.

Alone on an island,
Except the things I hear.
Wolves howling in the wind,
Making me shiver with fear.

Alone on an island,
Except the things I smell.
The burning of my fire,
I want someone to tell . . .

Alone on an island,
How I miss my mum.
And wish that she were here with me,
To make this seem like fun.

Alone on an island,
I really want to scream.
Suddenly I wake up,
And realise it's just a dream.

**Paige Anthony (9)**
**Engayne Primary School, Upminster**

# I Hate . . .

I do not like English,
It's too boring,
Reading stories that are good are not,
We have to do this every morning.

I do not like mathematics as well,
Division especially,
I can't do any more fractions,
My teacher says I don't think wisely.

I dislike those two but also science is dumb,
They don't know how many planets there are,
Making ice melt is a waste of time,
They even do experiments with Mars bars!

I do not like history or the word,
I would like Henry VIII to execute it,
Why are the Romans called Romans?
History for me is quits!

Also I hate D&T,
(Design and Technology),
Torches are not useful in any way,
I am sick of the name D&T!

If I hate D&T,
Of course I would hate art,
Especially when we . . .

*Hold on a useless boring minute!*
*I love art!*

I do like art,
I cannot think of anything better,
I am going to get a paintbrush,
To paint a letter.

**Faheem Kirefu  (9)**
**Gearies Junior School, Ilford**

# Whale Life

I am a whale lost at sea,
I'm almost extinct like my poor family.
I'm always so lonely, no one to see,
There's a little fish, it always calls me.
I think it's annoying it always talks to me.
I have a new home at the bottom of the sea.
There I found lots of animals like me.
I can see a lot of good food to eat,
It looks like some tasty treats.
Now I have new friends and a new home,
What more could I have?

**Ayesha Kiani (10)**
**Meadfurlong Middle School, Milton Keynes**


# Insane Wayne

There was a little boy called Wayne,
who used to drive me insane,
I ran from the classroom screaming,
while he was on the floor doing the cleaning.

I put my hand up and said, 'Please Miss, can I move instead?'
'No,' said the teacher, 'you can stay there.'
Next he was driving me around the bend,
Just like it would never end.
So the teacher got fed up with Wayne
and moved me one place next to Kane.

**Serena Robb (10)**
**Meadfurlong Middle School, Milton Keynes**

# Lion!

Lion is like a massive cat,
Eyes are bright torches,
Claws are like sharp knives,
Teeth are gleaming white.

Hunting his prey day and night,
The forest of trees as a jungle,
Its fur bushy as candyfloss,
Ready to attack.

Stalking dangerously but quietly,
Like a little mouse,
He keeps out of sight.

**Anna Krajinska (10)**
**Meadfurlong Middle School, Milton Keynes**


# Motorbikes

Motorbike I see you zoom by,
faster than a bird soaring in the sky.
Your engine's raging like a bull
make sure your petrol's full.
Wheels spin faster than a top
make sure the tyres don't flop.
Please make sure you don't crash
or the rider will have a nasty bash.

**Daniel Jones (10)**
**Meadfurlong Middle School, Milton Keynes**

# The Volcano

I was tall and proud of it
Rocky, hard and very crumbly
I used to spit out molten lava
Covering hundreds of miles of land
Red-hot goo
Spurted out from above me
Whenever I was ready
It would just happen
Like that.

Now all I am is a crumbly crater
No more spitting out goo from above me
People coming to visit me
Every day hundreds of people treading on me
Taking pictures of me
*Flash, flash, flash.*

I have more people come visit me now I am dead
Than when I was alive
No one came near me when I was alive
Even though they are above me I feel quite alone
Although everyone is here
I don't know why they like me more
Now I am dead.

I will stay here smoking
For the rest of my time.

**Lucy Harris (10)**
**Meadfurlong Middle School, Milton Keynes**

# The Birds

When it's a sunny day
The birds come out to play
When they start to flutter their wings
They come out to sing.

Come out sun
Then we will have fun
You will burn
We will learn.

Their nest is neat
When they eat
They eat lots of worms
When the sunset burns.

When the wind blows
The birds start to slow
When they're in their nest
They look their best.

When they have some chicks
They start to gather sticks
They will start to smell
If they don't wash really well.

They're in the tree
So let them be.

**Kerry Vanmeer Sheridan & Abigail Kisimisi  (9)**
**Meadfurlong Middle School, Milton Keynes**

# What Is White?

White is the colour of snow on Christmas Eve,
Like a baby's book with no colour
And like fresh, new paper on a work desk,
White is the cotton clouds floating in the sky,
The hard chalk on a blackboard.

White is the colour of lilies on a shelf,
Like milk pouring out of its jug,
White is the brightness of a freshly painted room,
White is the tip of a cotton bud, fresh and soft.

White is the colour of the twinkling stars at night,
Like tired eyes looking at the sun,
White is the colour of icing on a Christmas cake,
White is the colour of the moon glowing and fresh.

**Jodie Russell  (10)**
**Meadfurlong Middle School, Milton Keynes**


# What Is Grey?

What is grey?
Grey is as dark as a rainy day,
Grey is the wind that blew your hat away,
Grey is the colour of twilight and dusk,
Grey is the word you use if you must.

Grey is the colour that makes the trees sway,
Grey is the word to describe the squirrels
that lay in a nest of branches, twigs and hay,
Grey is the feeling at bay
when death and destruction are on their way,
Grey is the colour of shock and dismay.

**Nikita Hayward  (10)**
**Meadfurlong Middle School, Milton Keynes**

# The Seasons

In the autumn
The leaves rustle in the wind
The cold leaves come off the trees
In their mixed colours.

In the winter
The trees lose their leaves
Christmas comes and snowdrops come down
Children play in the snow

In the spring
The sun starts to peek in
And shine on the plants
Daffodils start to spread all over like a yellow blanket.

In the summer
The plants start blooming in the sun
Birds sing, children play and seas calm in the waves
And gardens start to fill with colours.

But these have to come to an end
So a new season will live and new life will come.

**Amar Shamji (11)**
**Meadfurlong Middle School, Milton Keynes**


# It

It was huge with bright eyes,
It looked like it had eaten a load of pies.
It was pink with little floppy ears,
It was with its friends who had big rears.
It looked like they had had a big dig,
Guess what it was, it was a great pink pig.

**Ellie Brudenell (10)**
**Meadfurlong Middle School, Milton Keynes**

# Why Did I Pick This School?

See me through the translucent windowpane
Crying in sympathy, this is loss of my life
Falling tears from windowed eyes
How could we be so strong?
Loving our parents with all our hearts
While the others all play darts.

Hang on, what's that on what? What's going on?
Confusion is the main object - everywhere.
All I see is the comings upon me.
I sit and stand in the hall,
As if there's no doctors on call.

Why oh why did I pick this school?
It's terrible.

**Anneke Hurley (10)**
**Meadfurlong Middle School, Milton Keynes**


# The Night

Night is as comforting as your cuddly toy
She walks over hills and down past streams
Her face is like treacle, it makes your heart melt.

When dawn defeats her she clambers down into her
underground home
And sleeps till eve comes out
She blows and stars shoot out and light up the sky.

With sleek black hair and light blue eyes
She's as beautiful as a butterfly
Night is as comforting as your cuddly toy
But she can be evil . . .

**Joanna Clark (10)**
**R A Butler Junior School, Saffron Walden**

# Ruler Of The Night

As the night eats day
He swoops out his gloomy, starry cloak
Darkness suddenly takes over the world
As dark, as dark as coal
As the destructive night strolls around
He blacks out the sun
A dark and misty face
As cold as ice
And black murky eyes
The bright red lips and yellow teeth
Threaten you to go outside
The bald, shiny head
Is the twinkling moon
The ruler of night
Is back again.

**Sonia Coates (10)**
**R A Butler Junior School, Saffron Walden**


# Night-Time

Night haunts you from the moment you shut your eyes
Looking at the clock waiting till morning
Night is still and scary like a slithering snake
Night is as lonely as a graveyard
Only with an evil skeleton's spirit
Night makes people scream till sunrise
Night's face has deep red eyes surrounded by a deep black outline
His hair is black with blond sharp spikes
Night lives in a deep, dark place
Find out before it haunts you!

**Fraser Parry (10)**
**R A Butler Junior School, Saffron Walden**

# Night Is A Living Being

When you shut your eyes,
A pair open,
Two stars appear in the sky,
These eyes belong to a woman,
Named Night.

Night is cold-blooded,
She's scary and haunting,
Makes you feel threatened and weak,
Gives you nightmares,
She's like a burglar,
Invisible against the dark sky.

Night makes the werewolves whine,
The wind whistle,
Her face is old,
But she isn't ageing,
She's been haunting people since time began.

Her mouth is the moon,
Her hair is long and dark,
Swaying along the rooftops,
A cloak is worn that covers the sun,
A dress she wears also that contains the bright stars.

Night's movement is graceful,
She leaps from chimney to chimney,
Star to star,
Night lives in the Arctic,
As no one ever enters that island.

So remember,
When you shut your eyes,
A pair open,
Two stars appear in the sky,
These women belong to a woman,
Named Night.

**Annabel Gammack (10)**
**R A Butler Junior School, Saffron Walden**

# Twilight Zone

Night is as nasty as a howling ghost, destroying all peace.
Everybody's nightmares rolling in like a river of hell.
Petrifying crashes in one room and a strange voice
almost like a ghost or a big, scary burglar stealing all possessions,
like a hurricane it lifts and blows away all hope and peace,
like Hell, nothing goes right.
Night is as nasty as a howling ghost destroying all peace.

**Bethany Brown  (11)**
**R A Butler Junior School, Saffron Walden**


# Apples

Down with the apples
They never should be ate
And if they were and if they were
They'd back up I bet.

Down with the apples
The poison lies beneath
My granddad bit a hard one once
And it pulled out all his teeth.

Down with the apples
But Mother disagrees
She eats them after breakfast
And eats them with her cheese.

Up with the chocolates
Up with the sweets
But for my little apples
I will never, never eat.

**Alice Marks  (10)**
**R A Butler Junior School, Saffron Walden**

# Night

When you drift off to sleep,
Night takes a pounce,
He scratches and scrapes in your brain,
Snatching all your happy dreams,
And replacing them with nightmares,
Stabbing into your head like a knife cutting bread.

Night has eyes,
Staring down and yet never blinking,
His cloak is ebony-black just like the night sky,
It flows to the ground and rustles with the wind,
He pounces on stars at dawn like a tiger to its prey,
In fear of seeing the blinding light of the sun,
He hides behind the planets at day.

**Zoë Maskell (10)**
R A Butler Junior School, Saffron Walden


# What Is The Point?

What is the point in owning a dog
if you never walk it?

What is the point of owning a cat
if you never let it in the house?

What is the point of owning a rabbit
if you never feed it?

What is the point of owning a horse
if you never ride it?

What is the point in owning a pet
if you never look after it?

**Ella Hampson (10)**
R A Butler Junior School, Saffron Walden

# Night

Night is a harmlessly grumpy old man,
He wraps you in his warmest blanket while sobbing
Softly for his lost family.
Night is as caring as a solitary dove lost far away
From its friends,
Night's face is as wrinkled as a discarded ball of paper
In the gutter.
He's been there since time began!
His eyes are like a hawk's,
Protecting us from evil perils.

He has a kind mouth speaking only the kindest, softest words,
He wears a tattered all stripy nightgown,
Night moves slowly like a friendly old ghost,
Night is very comforting, he loves everybody.

Night watches over you till dawn awakes!

**Florence Davis (10)**
**R A Butler Junior School, Saffron Walden**


# Night Poem

Night is like a devil,
Waiting for the moment,
He waits until his prey's asleep,
And then he pounces, quick as a whip.
He sends his mind deep into yours,
And gives you nightmares you'll never forget.
His face is old and wrinkled,
Stares you in the eyes,
Until you fall into his grasp.

**Oliver Moktar (10)**
**R A Butler Junior School, Saffron Walden**

# Alone

Stiff arms in the air,
The wind has made no effort at all.
Once, she was a cheerful thing,
With leaves at her feet,
Now she is dead, but she is
Far too big, to go in a grave.
No one grieves for her, she has no friends.
Her feet are big, but no one can see them,
Her torso is smooth, with rough bits
That catch on your fingers.
In the winter, she looks the same as other trees,
But her heart stands still, very still.

**Emily Cooke (9)**
**R A Butler Junior School, Saffron Walden**


# Anger

Anger is like a red-hot exploding volcano
When the burning lights dance,
Anger smells like smoke from a burning oven
Destroying everything in its way,
Anger sounds like a drum beating
Very slowly, sounding spooky,
Anger tastes like red-hot chilli peppers
That burn your tongue,
Anger feels like the Devil is burning you
With his Devil stick,
Anger reminds me of a person jumping into
Red-hot lava, burning their skin dying
Slowly and painfully.

**Adam Oukhellou (9)**
**Roydon Primary School, Roydon**

# Fear

Fear is the colour of the black-grey sky,
It sounds like tumbling rocks crashing together,
It tastes like red-hot chilli pepper,
It looks like a little boy getting told off,
It feels like my mum getting very, very angry,
It reminds me of something that I don't want to happen.

**Tommy Smithson  (7)**
Roydon Primary School, Roydon


# Anger

Anger is red, like an erupting volcano.
It sounds like waves crashing at the shore.
It tastes like a glass of lava.
It looks like smoke rushing out of your ears.
It feels like a needle going through your face.
It reminds me of a devil eating you.

**Matthew Wellbeloved  (7)**
Roydon Primary School, Roydon


# Hate

Hate is blacky-blue, like the night sky,
Hate sounds like the noise from a fierce dragon,
Hate tastes like a cabbage in a hot fire,
Hate looks like a stinging nettle with an angry face,
Hate feels like noisy tigers roaring,
Hate reminds me of dead people turning into ghosts.

**Stefan Losi  (7)**
Roydon Primary School, Roydon

# Fear

Fear is black, like the night,
Fear sounds like a growl from the spooky night,
Fear tastes like some blood from a vampire's jaw,
Fear looks like a claw from a devil on our floor,
Fear feels like some wolves fighting in your heart,
Fear reminds me of the fear running in my heart.

**Sam Harding (7)**
Roydon Primary School, Roydon


# Love

Love is like pink roses falling from the sky,
It sounds like long grass swishing low and high,
Love tastes like a juicy orange rolling to and fro,
It looks like a land far and by,
Love feels like squeezing a sponge when you feel shy,
It reminds me of Valentine's Day . . .

**Rachel Hedger (7)**
Roydon Primary School, Roydon


# Love

Love is light pink, like two lips getting together,
It sounds like two lovebirds singing in their tree,
Love tastes of Chinese, fresh out of the oven,
It looks like a heart with an arrow through it,
Love feels like two hands holding each other,
It reminds me of the first kiss I ever had.

**Dana Bailey McLean (7)**
Roydon Primary School, Roydon

# Anger

Anger is red, like the hot, burning heart burning,
It smells like a smoking crop farm,
Anger tastes like a burnt Sunday roast,
It sounds like a huge, shaking, earth-splitting earthquake,
Anger feels like an army attacking you from all sides,
With no chance to get away,
It reminds me of buildings being demolished,
With great force and emotional sounds.

**Matthew Hedger (9)**
**Roydon Primary School, Roydon**


# Happiness

Happiness is the colour of bright yellow, gleaming like the sun,
It sounds like birds singing in a tree,
Happiness tastes like bright red strawberries, clean and ripe to pick,
Happiness looks like beautiful white roses shedding their petals,
Happiness feels like cuddles with warm hands,
Happiness reminds me of kisses before bed.

**Amy Hagues (7)**
**Roydon Primary School, Roydon**


# Anger

Anger is red, like a red-hot chilli pepper exploding in my mouth,
Smelling like a blaze of smoke coming very close,
Sounds like an exploding volcano and
Tastes like a bowl of hot sauce,
It feels like a burning fire sizzling all around me,
It reminds me of a naughty, evil little devil laughing in my face.

**Zoe Gasson (10)**
**Roydon Primary School, Roydon**

# Happiness

Happiness is a rainbow stretched across the sea,
Or it's a pot of gold shimmering within me.
Magic magenta is its colour of pure truth,
Happiness feels like God helping you with your tooth,
It feels like fleece as soft as very much alive hair,
Happiness is the sun spreading it everywhere,
When you hear happiness, it sounds like birds singing,
It smells like roses with their lively insides ringing,
Tasting like pie is happiness in every last bite,
Happiness is a good thing so don't try its might.

**Samantha McLean (10)**
Roydon Primary School, Roydon


# Anger

Red as a trickle of fresh red blood,
A car revving a rusty engine,
Like fire burning cold, lonely branches,
Taste of smelly, burnt, black piece of toast,
People fight in the middle of streets,
Bacon burning in a frying pan,
Volcano launching out red lava.

**Jamie Parker (11)**
Roydon Primary School, Roydon


# Love

Love is red like a red rose,
Love sounds like dripping rain,
It tastes like a fruity strawberry,
Love looks like a big pink flower,
Love feels like a cute fluffy kitten,
It reminds me of big silver stars.

**Emma Abbey (7)**
Roydon Primary School, Roydon

# Hatred

The colour is dark red, like blood dripping from a murdered body,
It sounds like a newborn baby that never stops screaming,
It feels cold and contaminated with a deadly disease,
It tastes mouldy, disgusting like milk left in a fridge for ages,
It looks like a volcano about to explode with you on it,
It smells like a dead animal with flies plucking at its raged heart,
It reminds me of a human being, being hated by someone
That's worse than them.

**Connor Cranmer  (11)**
**Roydon Primary School, Roydon**


# Love

Love smells like a flowery perfume,
Love is as red as a thorny rose in a lovely garden,
Love sounds like a heart beating faster and faster,
Love tastes like a fluffy pink marshmallow,
Love feels like a really cute puppy just being born,
Love looks like a diamond wedding ring shimmering,
Love reminds me of my rabbit hopping around its hutch.

**Lucy Hancock  (8)**
**Roydon Primary School, Roydon**


# Love

Red is the colour of people in love,
It sounds like love music playing above,
Feels like romantic people sitting there,
Tastes like chocolate being eaten with care,
It looks sweet when two people are kissing,
Smells like flowers that people are picking,
Reminds me of newborn puppies sleeping,
It looks nice when two people are weeping.

**Yazmin Oukhellou  (10)**
**Roydon Primary School, Roydon**

# Love

Love is like a very bright red rose growing from the ground,
Love looks like my hamster standing on his two back
legs looking at me,
Love tastes like a very big pancake with lots of sugar on top,
Love smells like my mum's roast dinner cooking in the oven,
Love feels like a hamster's fur coat,
Love sounds like a dolphin jumping in and out of the sea,
Love reminds me of my hamster Sniff, running in his ball
going into things.

**Connie Maunder (8)**
**Roydon Primary School, Roydon**


# Love

Love is like a red bushy rose,
Love looks like two people dancing in the air,
Love smells like a fresh juicy strawberry,
Love sounds like a violin playing softly,
Love feels like a baby playing independently,
Love tastes like a juicy red apple,
Love reminds me of a red heart with angels flying around it.

**Francesca Baldry (9)**
**Roydon Primary School, Roydon**


# Hunger

It makes you think of tasty food,
It tastes just like a fresh air pie, ...
It puts you in an angry mood,
Even when you're about to die,
It looks like a mouldy old room,
When it's filled with dirty water,
Smells like bristles of an old broom,
Even though it's just like slaughter.

**Gordon (11)**
**Roydon Primary School, Roydon**

# To Make A Christmas Cake

To make a Christmas cake I need:
2 eggs,
4oz flour,
4oz butter,
4oz raisins,
4oz currants,
2oz nuts
1 lemon
And a dash of whiskey,
Then I can make a Christmas cake.

First crack 2 eggs into a bowl,
Then add 4oz of flour,
And 4oz of butter,
And mix it together with your hands,
Sample the whiskey to check its quality,
Add the raisins,
Check the whiskey,
Add the currants,
Check the whiskey,
Don't waste the whiskey on the cake, drink it yourself,
Then crack the lemon, and strain your nuts,
Mix on the turnerer,
Check the whiskey,
Don't forget the turnerer,
Throw the bowl out of the window,
Go to bed,
Nobody likes Christmas cake anyway.

**Daniel Hodges  (10)**
**St Edward's CE Primary School, Romford**

# Winter

Winter is a wonderland,
The snow covers the cars like a duvet of snow,
Winter is the best season because you can make
Snowmen and have time off school because
Of the bad weather,
Then you have the best time of your life
And wait for Santa Claus.

**Emma Flynn (10)**
St Edward's CE Primary School, Romford

# Sport

Rugby - my favourite sport,
Rugby - a sport for boys,
Sport is healthy,
Sport is fun,
Sport makes you run,
Jonny plays sport,
Jonny is great,
John Cena beat Booker T.

**Andrew Lawrence (10)**
St Edward's CE Primary School, Romford

# Pets And Animals

Little girls and little boys have cuddly cats,
Scurrying rats,
Dribbling dogs,
Spiky hedgehogs,
Talking parrots,
Rabbits eating carrots,
There are many pets and there can be many more,
So that's it for you, can you think of any more?

**Sophie Bannis (10)**
St Edward's CE Primary School, Romford

# Birthdays

Birthdays are fun,
Sweets and chocolate,
Some have music,
And flashing lights,
Some are swimming,
Playing on all the floats,
But best of all are sleepovers,
Telling ghost stories,
Too frightened to go to sleep,
Watching DVDs and eating popcorn,
Hiding in our sleeping bags,
When it comes to morning, we are too tired to tidy,
Birthdays are the best ever!

**Harriet Greenhill  (10)**
St Edward's CE Primary School, Romford


# Chestnut

Chestnut sweet chestnut,
To pick up and eat or keep
Until winter,
When hot they're a treat,
It's hard and prickly outside
And silky in where little nuts hide.

**Russell Meddings  (11)**
St Edward's CE Primary School, Romford


# Summer Haiku

Summer's very hot,
It is a scorching season,
It is the *greatest!*

**Joshua Steer  (10)**
St Edward's CE Primary School, Romford

# Snow

The snow fell down hard,
It covered all the cars,
Children playing in it happy and joyful,
All the children going 'Ohh' because it is so beautiful,
The snow fell like a dust of wind,
The snow all around.

It will go by tomorrow,
So play in it now,
It will be gone soon.

**Emma Isbell (10)**
**St Edward's CE Primary School, Romford**


# Disco

The flash of the light,
The swish of the record,
The DJ's voice,
The sound of music,
The boom of the bass,
What am I?

**Edwad Guest (10)**
**St Edward's CE Primary School, Romford**


# Fair

Roller coasters zooming round and round,
Wrappers and packets thrown on the ground,
Soft and fluffy candyfloss on sticks,
Funny clowns doing mad tricks,
Ferris wheels and haunted houses,
Toys, gifts and prizes,
It's so much fun at the fair.

**Chloë Herring (11)**
**St Edward's CE Primary School, Romford**

# How To Make A . . . Boyfriend

To make a boyfriend
All you do is simply take,
6oz of charm,
9oz of passion,
9oz of 6 packs,
10oz of gorgeous looks,
7oz of intelligence,
9kg of love for you,
6oz of attention for you,
8oz of cheekiness,
9kg of hugs and kisses,
7oz of remembering your birthday,
5oz of money,
Now you have your ingredients
Put them together like so,
Mix it all together slowly
And watch the passion bubble,
Then put the mixture in the oven for 20 minutes
And watch your dream guy rise.

**Elizabeth Portsmouth (10)**
St Edward's CE Primary School, Romford

# What Friendship Means

Friendship brings true happiness,
In winter, friends can gather round you,
In spring, friends can take cover on a cold raining day,
In summer friends will help you when in need,
In fall, you and your friends can share lots of laughter,
But mostly a friend is someone who thinks you are nicest of all,
Friends are loyal and true and they care about you
In winter, spring, summer and fall,
A person who has friends must himself/herself be friendly,
But be a friend who sticks closer than a brother or sister.

**Naomi Babalola (10)**
St Edward's CE Primary School, Romford

# Winter

Winter is white, like a big fluffy duvet,
It feels like you've got frostbite on your little toes,
It smells like a blast of fresh air coming off the sea,
It sounds like it's snowing very heavily indeed,
It looks like a white snowy duvet,
It tastes like water is spraying on your taste buds,
It reminds you of going on holiday, a skiing holiday.

**Emily Higgs (10)**
St Edward's CE Primary School, Romford


# My Poem

I am the cheekiest of the jungle,
I am obviously cheeky,
I have a long tail like a snake,
I use it to swing from tree to tree,
I am brown and furry like a woolly jumper,
I have small human-like hands for eating with.
Who am I?

**Claire Tibbott (10)**
St Edward's CE Primary School, Romford


# Birthday Party

Whatever you do don't have a party like this,
There were food bombs exploding,
Children screaming even the parents were losing it,
The children popping balloons, it was anybody's nightmare,
Wherever the children were, there was chaos,
When the cake came out which was chocolate,
It was smudged on every child's face,
At the end, all the children
Were asleep that's the only advantage!

**Lois Holmes (10)**
St Edward's CE Primary School, Romford

# A Puzzle

I am beautiful, bright colours,
I only come out when the sky
Is both rainy and sunny,
I am really pretty when I am out,
I am famous for a story in the Bible,
That is about me,
Some people say a leprechaun has a pot
Of gold over the other side of me.
What am I?

**Leanne Walker (10)**
St Edward's CE Primary School, Romford

# Spring

Spring is a bright yellow,
It tastes like a bar of chocolate,
It looks like swans swimming gracefully,
It smells like the scent of gardens where the rain's been falling,
It sounds like a flute playing,
It reminds me of the warm, golden sun.

**Charlotte Ross (10)**
St Edward's CE Primary School, Romford

# My World

My head hits the pillow
I'm in my world again.
Flowers sway in the breeze,
I'm in my world again.
No family or friends
I'm in my world again.
Rabbits and foxes dance and prance
I'm in my world again.
My alarm goes off
I'm in the real world again.

**Rachel Vallance (11)**
St Edward's CE Primary School, Romford

# Football

The ref's blown the whistle,
The match has begun,
Man U boot it up to Rooney,
He dribbles the ball,
Does a couple of backflips,
Shoots and he oh, he's missed!
Oh well, there goes Arsenal down
The wing to Reyes,
He shoots, he scores!

Man U are coming back,
It's 1-0 and Paul Scholes has
The ball, he passes it to Rooney
And he scores, 1-1.
The end c′ ˙ʰe FA Cup Final
And it's 1-1, guess what they
Have to do with the cup?
Cut it in
   *Half!*

**Melanie Marsden (10)**
St Edward's CE Primary School, Romford


# Swimming

Swimming is the best, you never need a rest,
Front crawl, backstroke, breast and fly,
Learn to swim and you won't die.

Up and down, to and fro, see how far that you can go.
Front crawl, backstroke, breast and fly,
Learn to swim and you won't die.

Don't watch telly, don't just sit,
Let's go swimming, let's get fit,
Front crawl, backstroke, breast and fly,
Learn to swim and you won't die.

**Kayleigh Gibbs (10)**
St Edward's CE Primary School, Romford

# Volcano

The rumbling and
Magnificent destruction
Of the noisy fire.

The erupting of the
Lava surge erupts
Around the neighbourhood.

It is a natural
Instinct to nature
And eats whatever
It can in its way.

The volcano erupts
And settles down.
The gushing and
Rumbling ceases.
All is quiet, peaceful
And still.

**Jonathan Sheppard (10)**
**St Edward's CE Primary School, Romford**


# Families

We have a big family, there's 11 of us,
We can't fit in a car, so we use a minibus,
We have 6 boys, 3 girls, a mum, a dad too,
But unfortunately we only have 1 loo,
We have 3 dogs, a rabbit, a hamster and a cat,
But they don't wipe their feet on the doormat,
They spread mud around the house,
The cat thinks the hamster is a mouse.

**Paris Parnell (10)**
**St Edward's CE Primary School, Romford**

# The Seasons

Spring is full of lambs,
Easter is this time of year,
Spring is warming up.

The children leave school,
They all go on holiday,
Summer is today.

Harvest is here again,
The children are back at school,
Hallowe'en is near.

Advent's near Xmas,
Christmas on the 25th,
Hey! It's a new year!

Life is a circle,
From spring round until winter,
Here we go again!

**Jonathan Neale  (10)**
**St Edward's CE Primary School, Romford**


# Cricket

The bowler bowls it,
It speeds down the lawn,
The batsman's tricked, *out!*
The umpire puts his hand up,
He reckons the batsman's out.

The next batsman's ready,
The bowler bowls it right on stumps,
*Crack,* the ball hits the wood,
It flies towards the boundary,
It goes into the crowd - *six*!

**Peter Sheppard  (10)**
**St Edward's CE Primary School, Romford**

# The Forest

The forest is full of creatures,
Either great or small,
They scuttle on the forest floor,
Behind trees big and small.

They run around in daytime
Looking for their food,
Finding nuts and fruit around
While birds sing and coo.

The ants run up and down the trees,
Scurrying and hurrying without a care,
They also collect dead twigs
To eat, enjoy and share.

The leaves on the trees rustle,
Their branches wave around,
If you ever go it's a pretty sight,
But don't make a sound.

**Lucy Waine  (10)**
**St Edward's CE Primary School, Romford**

# Colours

Pink is the flower, that sits in the vase,
Green is the long moss-covered grass,
Red is the flame, so hot and bright,
Yellow is the sun, that gives us light,
White is the snow, so crisp and cold,
Gold is the ring, so solid and bold,
Blue is the sky, that is over us all,
Orange is the tall, brick-built wall,
Purple is the plum, so small and ripe,
Black is Grandad's smoking pipe,
Rainbows you see when the rain's gone away,
These are the colours we see every day.

**Kirsty Chesney  (10)**
**St Edward's CE Primary School, Romford**

# Snow/Love

Snow is gentle also fragile,
You can play with it,
But sooner or later, it will melt,
The angel of snow is coming down,
You notice her,
Because you see a light coming down,
As bright as the sun she's fluent and calm,
You can notice her more when it's night,
She dances with him as he picks up a flower for her,
She smells it and then lets it go,
He loves her so much and sweet but not sour, you are.
Roses are red,
Violets are blue,
You are the one I will always love,
Cheery but not berry you are,
Soft as comfort,
I will cherish you like treasure,
Never shall we break up,
As the angel of snow so fluent and gentle,
She moves up into the sky with a shiny light,
Going with her, his last few words are I love you,
You're like a beautiful white dove, just like snow,
As he waves goodbye,
As a single snowflake lands on his hand,
So fragile and guess what - it melts.

**Tosin Olagundoye  (11)**
**St Edward's CE Primary School, Romford**


# Birthday

It sounds like party poppers and kids screaming,
It tastes like icing, sweets and cake,
It looks like colourful balloons and party bags in bright colours,
It feels like sticky fingers and sweets,
It reminds me of happiness.

**Paige Blackman  (10)**
**St Edward's CE Primary School, Romford**

# My Favourite Things

I like shopping, clothes and even shoes,
I like bands and pop stars but my favourite I can't choose,
I like birthdays, Christmases and sweets,
I like playing the keyboard because it has some really cool beats,
I like Saturday nights just chillin',
I also like dancing and singing,
I like listening to CDs - I really do,
But best of all I like my friends and you too.

**Amy Austin (10)**
St Edward's CE Primary School, Romford


# Happiness

Happiness is orange, like the happy summer sun,
It looks like healthy green grass growing on the land.
It tastes like chocolate melting in your mouth,
It feels like sand tickling my feet.
It sounds like adults having a great time,
It smells like fruits growing from other countries.
All of these things remind me of playing in the park.

**Bonnie Rayner (10)**
St Edward's CE Primary School, Romford


# Love

Love is red, like candyfloss,
It looks like Cupid pointing an arrow,
It tastes like a snowman in the cold,
It smells like perfume in my face,
It feels like chocolate melting in my hand,
It sounds like children singing a song,
It reminds me of happy moments.

**Paige Slade (10)**
St Edward's CE Primary School, Romford

# Seasons

I love the winter
Because we play in the snow,
We drink hot cocoa.

Playing in autumn,
Finding conkers is great fun,
Leaves falling off trees.

I love the summer,
No more school for six whole weeks,
We can play all day.

Flowers are growing,
Buds are popping everywhere,
Spring starts life again.

**Joanna Rainbird (10)**
**St Edward's CE Primary School, Romford**


# Emotions

When I feel happy
I shout and play with my friends
But I stop calmly.

When I feel nervous
I shake and shiver with fright,
It's fine in the end.

When I feel angry
I always stamp, scream and shout,
I go hot and red.

When I am quite sad
I want to be on my own,
Though company's nice.

**Bryony Clark (10)**
**St Edward's CE Primary School, Romford**

# Summer

Summer is like the sun rising,
It feels like love all around us,
It sounds like a new baby born,
It looks like the shining sun,
It smells like pretty flowers,
It tastes like freshly grown strawberries,
It reminds me of God.

**Victoria Walsh (10)**
St Edward's CE Primary School, Romford

# Winter

Winter is white as it shines in the night,
It feels like children playing in the snow,
It tastes like Christmas pudding in my mouth,
It looks like a table full of my family,
It smells like frosted rings,
It sounds like children singing Christmas carols,
But most of all it reminds me of all the good things
People have done for me.

**Katie Walker (10)**
St Edward's CE Primary School, Romford

# Anger!

Anger is ruby-red, like a raging bull,
It feels like losing your temper so badly, it gives you headaches,
It tastes like a boiled sweet not cracking in your mouth,
It looks like boiling lava burning everything in sight,
It smells like an earthquake erupting up your nose,
It sounds like gas is coming out of your ears
And reminds you; he is going to blow!

**Mitchell John (10)**
St Edward's CE Primary School, Romford

# Surprise

Surprise is orange, like an explosion,
It feels like a pinch on your finger,
It tastes like a hot chilli in a stirfry,
It looks like a wacky jack-in-a-box,
It smells like the scent of a bottom burp,
It sounds like the bursting of a balloon,
It reminds me of winning my trophies.

**Joshua Daly (10)**
**St Edward's CE Primary School, Romford**


# Winter

Winter is silver, like snowmen smiling,
It feels like the freezer door open,
It tastes like ice melting in your mouth,
It looks as if chocolate drops fall from the sky,
It smells like fresh milk spilling on the ground,
It sounds like fine sugar being poured,
It reminds me of me and my family playing in the snow.

**Faye Freeman (10)**
**St Edward's CE Primary School, Romford**


# Spring

Spring is colourful, like a red rose opening,
It feels like little lambs dancing,
It tastes like an ice cream sundae,
It looks like happy children playing,
It smells like chocolate cookies in the oven,
It sounds like baby horses galloping in the open air,
It reminds me of Easter.

**Marie Hawkins (10)**
**St Edward's CE Primary School, Romford**

# Winter

Winter means bad winds,
Lots of presents at Christmas,
Winter means snowballs.

People play with snow,
Snow as white as a barn owl,
Winter can be cold.

Rivers are frozen,
Stones are as cold as metal,
Snow as cold as ice.

Snow is everywhere,
Snow is melting to water
And then it's all gone.

**Jay Haxell (10)**
**St Edward's CE Primary School, Romford**


# Seasons

Spring is warm and fun,
The swans now swim gracefully,
The children are glad.

Out in the garden,
Now we go on holidays,
We love summer days.

The brown leaves fall down,
Walking on them makes them crunch,
This time of year's fun.

Now winter is here,
The snow is falling on me,
I think of Jesus.

**Rachel Jones (10)**
**St Edward's CE Primary School, Romford**

# Winter

Winter is white like glowing snow.
Winter sounds like the wind when it whistles.
Winter smells like Granny's warm apple pies with the sweet smell.

Winter tasies like a hot crispy Christmas dinner.
Winter feels like playing with a new Christmas toy.

Winter reminds me of the relaxing two weeks off school.
Winter looks cold with frost and glowing snow.

**Robert Lord (10)**
**St Edward's CE Primary School, Romford**


# Sunny Summer Days

Summer is great fun,
It is my favourite season,
Good time for a swim.

Mum and Dad like it,
My pussy cat likes summer too,
We like it, do you?

In summer we play,
We play and play all the time,
Summer can be hot.

Summer can be cold,
Summer is all temperatures,
But I do not care.

Summer is a stove,
It cuddles right up to me,
I wish it would stay.

**Eden Pickton (11)**
**St Edward's CE Primary School, Romford**

# Animals

Animals are very different,
Many have four legs,
Some have two
And some have none,
Animals are very different.

Animals eat different things,
Herbivores eat plants,
Carnivores eat meat,
Omnivores eat both,
Animals eat different things.

Animals live in different places,
Some live in Europe and Asia,
Some live in Australia or India,
Some live in Africa or America,
Animals live in different places.

Animals need protection,
The dodo and mammoth are extinct,
The tiger and rhino are rare,
Some may become rare,
Animals need protection.

Guess how this happened?
It's due to the most dangerous animal on the planet,
You and me!

**John Coombes (10)**
**St Edward's CE Primary School, Romford**

# Maths

Maths is fun,
Maths is numbers,
Counting on in tens,
Adding and taking away,
All different numbers.

**Charles Fancourt (7)**
**St Edward's CE Primary School, Romford**

# Upside Down

I woke one morning
And found I was upside down,
So I went downstairs
Walking on the ceiling,
And my mum said, 'Off the ceiling you naughty girl.'
So I said, 'Mum I can't!'
And then she started pulling me!
Then she pulled my hair off!
'Oh my! Go and see the doctor dear!'

So I went to see the doctor
And I waited half an hour,
Then when I was told to go through
He didn't even see me,
So I said, 'Look up doctor!'
Then he looked up and said, 'Will you get off my ceiling!'
So I said, 'I can't!'
So he said, 'Don't talk nonsense.'
Then he started to pull me too,
First my hair then my arms,
What is next?

**Rebecca Willson  (10)**
St Edward's CE Primary School, Romford


# Love

Love is like a pink cloud,
It feels like a pink fluffy pillow.
Love tastes like a piece of candyfloss,
It looks like a pink teddy bear.
Love smells like a bottle of perfume,
It sounds like an angel singing.
Love reminds me of my holiday.

**Chelsey Morton  (10)**
St Edward's CE Primary School, Romford

# The Fair

The fair is here, 'Yes, hooray,'
And it's in the middle of May,
Lots of candyfloss here and there,
At first all I could do was look and stare,
Lots of rides whizzing around,
It was very loud, lots of sound,
I won a big teddy bear,
Soon my legs started to ache,
I wanted to sit on a chair,
I saw my favourite ride,
I ran up to it and got inside,
The day soon ended, I was very happy,
It came to bedtime
And I cuddled my new bear, Pappy.

**Amber Robins (10)**
**St Edward's CE Primary School, Romford**

# Animals

Say hello to the ginger cat
And just ignore the dark black bat.
All the dogs are barking
While all the cats are miaowing.
The apes are swinging
And the chimps are scratching.
The zoo animals are making all the noise
And you can see the long necks of the giraffes
When you open up your eyes.

**Siân Lloyd (10)**
**St Edward's CE Primary School, Romford**

# God Made Penguins

God made penguins
Minus knees
And filled them all with antifreeze.

God made penguins
Nice and small
So they can glide to the shopping mall.

God made penguins
With smooth bellies
And their flippers feel like jelly.

God made penguins,
He made them all
Large and small.

**Rufus Devine (10)**
St Edward's CE Primary School, Romford


# Rain

The rain is running down,
There is a splashing sound.
The clouds scatter drops of rain,
Now I've got a rusty bike frame.

The clouds frowned at me,
The rain fell on the tree.
Outside there was a shouting storm,
Inside my house it's very warm.

**Paul Braysher (11)**
St Edward's CE Primary School, Romford

# Dogs

Dogs are very loyal,
Some are very royal.

They like to play ball,
Everywhere even in the hall!

They play 'fetch' with sticks,
They give you big licks.

They sleep in your bed
And sit on your head!

They're your best pal,
When they're sad they howl!

They're there through thick and thin,
They eat out of everyone's bins.

They're your friends forever,
So don't neglect, abuse, starve or treat them wrong
And they will be with you all life long.

**Jade Taylor (11)**
**St Edward's CE Primary School, Romford**


# Winter - Haikus

Winter is coming,
It is my favourite season,
Winter will be here.

Christmas will be here,
People write their Christmas list
And there will be snow.

I am excited,
Presents underneath the tree,
Children are in bed.

**Alex Carter (10)**
**St Edward's CE Primary School, Romford**

# Animals

Animals have special feelings,
Like pigs, horses,
Even platypuses,
They all are animals that can feel,
Animals have special feelings.

Animals have special hearing
Because they are lower on the ground.
They can hear a lot of sounds,
If an enemy comes to eat they can hear them,
Animals have special hearing.

Animals have special homes,
Like moles, bats,
Even cats,
Crocodiles and fish live in water,
Animals have special homes.

**Kate Watson (10)**
**St Edward's CE Primary School, Romford**


# The Tale Of A Dragon

In a cave far away,
Dug in a mountainside,
Lives a dragon, great and fierce.

He sleeps on his mountain of treasure,
Taken from dwarves of old
And the gold glints in the moonlight.

His roar is magnified by the stone walls
And his throat spouted fire
And he circles, looking for the dwarves, revenge ever more.

**Martin Perchard (10)**
**St Edward's CE Primary School, Romford**

# Winter

Winter is coming soon,
It feels like freezing cold air which bites you,
It tastes like water from a fountain spraying water everywhere,
It looks like wool from a sheep gently falling down making
covers of snow,
It smells like white chocolate which makes us tempted to eat,
It sounds like people screaming in the night scared,
It reminds me that winter is the best season.

**Elliott Dark (10)**
St Edward's CE Primary School, Romford


# Winter

Winter is white, like a sheet of paper,
It feels like fluffy white clouds,
It tastes like Dream chocolate melting in your mouth,
It looks like a duvet warming you up,
It smells like fresh bread that's just been taken out of the oven,
It sounds like a bird singing,
It reminds me of all my friends.

**Rosie Abbott (10)**
St Edward's CE Primary School, Romford


# Fear

Fear is black like the black night sky,
It feels like icy hands creeping up your back,
It tastes like black smoke ready to choke you.
Fear looks like a black hole sucking everything up,
It smells like people's happiness being crushed to dust,
It sounds like crying people being surrounded by its darkness.
Fear reminds me of being scared.
Fear reminds me of scary nightmares.

**Aratope Ajose (10)**
St Edward's CE Primary School, Romford

# Stars

Stars are up there,
Up in the sky.

Do you look up there?
Sometimes there's one on its own
And some in a gang.
Sometimes there's a whole bunch.

But that's how life
Is isn't it?

When you are in bed,
Can you look out the window
And see them in the sky?
Some nights the clouds
Cover the shining stars.

But that's how life
Is isn't it?

**Katie Reeves  (10)**
**St Edward's CE Primary School, Romford**


# Thundering Anger

Thundering anger,
You are boiling over now,
Don't get too annoyed.

Your head is on fire,
Burning and blazing in rage,
Do not get angry.

Do not overflow,
Wait until this afternoon,
You will feel better.

Anger will now win,
You have to fight it off now
Or it will crush you.

**Joe Ambridge  (10)**
**St Edward's CE Primary School, Romford**

# Pandas

Pandas climb up trees,
They hate buzzy bees.
They have black and white fur
And they don't purr.
Pandas climb up trees,
They hate buzzy bees.
Some have blue eyes some have green,
Their eyes look kind not mean.
Pandas climb up trees,
They hate buzzy bees.
They have black squidgy noses
And they have sharp claws on their toesies.
Pandas climb up the trees,
They hate buzzy bees.
They eat bamboo sticks
And they always play tricks.
Pandas climb up trees,
They hate buzzy bees.
Pandas are cute and cuddly,
If you're kind they're all nice and snuffly.

**Poppy Small (10)**
**St Edward's CE Primary School, Romford**


# Winter

Winter is like the colours silver or gold,
It feels like a warm fire glowing and heating me up.
It tastes like a small chocolate inside your advent calendar
Because it has its own taste and its own day.
It looks like a dark night sky with lots of stars.
It smells like a pine cone or the Christmas tree
That has come down from the loft.
It sounds like the Christmas church bells ringing
And it reminds me of the birth of baby Jesus!

**Ruth Bannister (10)**
**St Edward's CE Primary School, Romford**

# Fruit

Strawberries are juicy and red,
The red goes right to my head.

Oranges are sweet and orange too,
They're good for me and you.

Bananas are pointy and yellow too,
Monkeys love them, do you?

Peaches are sour and make me quiver,
Their flesh all furry - oh! how I shiver.

Apples are hard, green and red,
I have one before I go to bed.

Grapes are juicy and green,
I think they're fit for the Queen.

Kiwis are green and furry too,
I like them, I hope you do.

**Hannah Maynard  (10)**
**St Edward's CE Primary School, Romford**


# Animals

Animals are *big,*
Animals are small,
Animals are sweet,
Animals are neat,
Animals glide,
Animals hide,
Animals care,
Animals dare,
Animals love you,
Animals hate you,
This is life's big circle,
I wonder why?

**Emma Johnson  (10)**
**St Edward's CE Primary School, Romford**

# The Night

The moon prances into the night,
Smiling down the street,
Watching children tucked in tight
Into their beds asleep.

Leaves on trees are silver,
The grass dances in the breeze,
In the distance is the river
Looking up at the trees.

The animals come out at night,
The owls go tu-whit tu-whoo,
The field mice scurry, quick in fright,
Back home, two by two.

When the clock strikes midnight
The air suddenly seems cold,
Pitch-black, no light
With stars that shine like gold.

**Mollie James (11)**
**St Edward's CE Primary School, Romford**


# Bike Race

Going down a hill,
Bumps and humps,
Bangs and crashes.

As you ride along, you fall
And have to limp on.

You recover quickly
And carry on,
Hooray! You've won!

**Robert Ward (10)**
**St Edward's CE Primary School, Romford**

# Books

Tales of exciting adventures
Or mysteries unsolved.
Bibles and other holy books
Or books in museums, covered with mould.
Tidy books and messy books,
School work books too,
Information books and fiction books.

More types than you ever knew.

Some people say reading's good for your brain,
I believe this is true.
Some people say reading's boring,
But I think people like this are few.
Small children have books that play music
And some people have books with music in,
Or just manuscript paper to write their own.

I've never seen any book thrown in the bin.

**Helen Smallwood  (11)**
**St Edward's CE Primary School, Romford**

# Christmas

Christmas is here,
Autumn has gone,
Santa is coming,
Jesus' light has shone.

Everyone is singing carols,
Everyone is getting nice presents,
The snow is falling from the sky
And Christmas time has been pleasant.

Christmas time is always great
And now the time has gone.

**Lauren Chesney  (10)**
**St Edward's CE Primary School, Romford**

# Christmas

The whole street is white,
All a very pretty sight,
Carol singers sing
As the church bells ring,
We decorate the Christmas tree,
Children playing is what we see,
The blazing in the home steals all night,
Waiting to see a shiny light,
Santa comes with big red suit,
Rudolph and his gang are very cute,
Christmas Day is here
And Christmas pudding is near,
We eat our lovely turkey
While I get pretty perky,
Christmas pudding is safe and sound in my tummy,
We are joking and being funny,
In bed I see the stars shining bright,
As I say goodnight,
My Christmas is over and we are back to spring.

**Sharmila Golan (10)**
**St Edward's CE Primary School, Romford**


# Stars

The stars twinkle in the sky
As my gran goes oh my, oh my.
They look so pretty in their skirts
While they cause a lot of mirth.
The sky is black, the stars are gold,
The weather is more than freezing cold.
The night has drawn in, the stars have come out,
They shine and twinkle like a roundabout,
Round and round, up and down,
Slowly spinning all around.
Silver, gold, what a lovely sight to behold.

**Oyinkan Oladapo (10)**
**St Edward's CE Primary School, Romford**

# The Pandas

Pandas are great,
Pandas are fun,
They play all day in the sun.

Pandas are fluffy,
Pandas are black and white,
All they do is chew all night.

Pandas are great,
Pandas are big
And when they eat they leave a twig
From all the bamboo.

Pandas are great,
Pandas are snugly,
They are wonderful creatures.

**Molly Scott  (10)**
**St Edward's CE Primary School, Romford**


# Dreams

I lay there thinking,
I get up and start drinking,
Why is it me?
Why am I thinking of this wonderful dream?
Why am I dreaming of apple trees,
Dancing and twirling and shaking their leaves.
Why am I dreaming of sunny days,
And going to the beach and finding caves.
Why am I dreaming of sailing a boat?
Then when it comes to shore I row it once more,
And when I wake up I am relieved
And I could not believe.

**Ross Anderson  (10)**
**St Edward's CE Primary School, Romford**

# The A To L Of Animals

A is for ant that scuttles away,
B is for buffalo that is very strong,
C is for cheetah which is very speedy,
D is for dog which is very energetic,
E is for elephant which is big and large,
F is for fox that comes out at night,
G is for goldfish that swims around,
H is for Himalayan blue bear which is higher than anywhere,
I is for iguana fat and slow,
J is for jaguar slim and fast,
K is for kangaroo kicking everything,
L is for leopard climbing trees.

**Christian Smith  (10)**
**St Edward's CE Primary School, Romford**


# Chocolate

Can I have a chocolate Mum?
Only something small, yum-yum,
Mars bar is a bit too small,
Milky Way is OK,
Magic Stars lots, but little,
Caramel, two but tiny,
I suppose there is only one left,
The super duper Dairy Milk,
Please Mum I'll eat my dinner.

**Maria Howard  (10)**
**St Edward's CE Primary School, Romford**


# The Dragon - Haiku

People fight dragons,
They killed all of them but one,
But they never won.

**Chester Reginald Garnish (10)**
**St Edward's CE Primary School, Romford**

# Sadness

When someone makes you cry
You have to wave bye-bye.

When someone hurts your feelings
Or steals from your dad's shop,
What will you do to make it stop?

If someone says a swear word
Just don't listen to their word.

If someone's being horrible
Don't be horrible back.

If someone's being unkind
Don't be unkind back.

**Samuel Kelly (7)**
**St Edward's CE Primary School, Romford**


# I Love Maths

Two eyes,
One nose,
Ten toes,
One head,
Five fingers,
One book of maths.

**Teniayo Dare (7)**
**St Edward's CE Primary School, Romford**


# Maths

2+2 are 4 cats.
4+4 are 8 flat tyres.
6+6 are 12 rats.
8+8 are 16 mats.

**Jonathan Petre (7)**
**St Edward's CE Primary School, Romford**

# Sadness

When someone makes you cry
You have to say goodbye.

When someone falls over you
Help, be kind, not unkind.

Hurting other people's feelings is very, very bad,
Don't hurt other people's feelings.

**Philip Hawkins  (7)**
St Edward's CE Primary School, Romford


# My Pet Leopard Gecko

Long climber,
Fast mover,
Scaly skin,
Cricket eater,
Sharp claws,
Yellow body with black spots,
Brown eyes,
My pet leopard gecko.

**Dominic Phillips  (7)**
St Edward's CE Primary School, Romford


# Money

I've got a whole purse of it at home,
Then I spend it all day long.
I love money,
It's the best in the whole world.

**Millie Parnell  (7)**
St Edward's CE Primary School, Romford

# Sadness

When someone makes you cry
You have to wave bye-bye.

When someone hurts your feelings
Or steals from your dad's shop
What will you do to make it stop?

If someone says a swear word
Just don't listen to their word.

If someone's being horrible don't be horrible back,
If you do you feel like you're going to crack.

If someone's being unkind
Don't be unkind back.

**Matthew Lloyd  (7)**
**St Edward's CE Primary School, Romford**


# Money

Money, I spend my money in 4 minutes,
I love money, it is so good to have,
I have got a house full of it today
And I've got some now in my car
And my car is made of money
And money is the best.

**Nina Hajittof  (7)**
**St Edward's CE Primary School, Romford**


# Angels

Angels are caring,
Angels are watching in the sky.
Angels are looking down on you
To make sure you're safe
And to make sure you're not in danger.

**Kerrie Norris  (7)**
**St Edward's CE Primary School, Romford**

# Maths

Maths is cool,
Maths is fun,
Maths is good
For everyone.

Maths is fun,
Maths is cool,
Maths is good
For every school.

Maths is fun,
Maths is good
For everyone.

Maths is cool,
Maths is good
For every school.

Maths is good,
Maths is good,
If you hate maths
You still should.

**Libby Dejoodt  (7)**
**St Edward's CE Primary School, Romford**


# Happiness

Happiness is yellow, like a sunflower,
It looks like romance in a restaurant,
It sounds like music playing,
It feels like the sea water touching me,
It tastes like an angel from God,
It smells like dinner cooking right now,
It reminds me of my mum's anniversary.

**Luke Reeve  (7)**
**St Edward's CE Primary School, Romford**

# Sadness

I wish I could stop being sad, miserable and blue,
But I just do not know how to.
I would like to stop being horrible to people,
But sometimes they really make me cross.

**Jessica Chesney  (7)**
St Edward's CE Primary School, Romford


# Love

Love is red like blood,
It sounds like music to my ears,
It looks like pink in the sky,
It reminds me of happiness.

**Jake Farmer  (7)**
St Edward's CE Primary School, Romford


# Shapes

Twist, turn, jump and play,
Makes shapes
With your body each day.

**Folasade Cline-Thomas  (7)**
St Edward's CE Primary School, Romford


# Happiness

Happiness is yellow, like the shining sun,
It smells like yellow sunflowers in your garden,
It feels like somewhere in my heart,
It looks like the sun coming down to dance with me,
It looks like my head on my body.

**Elizabeth Hawkins  (7)**
St Edward's CE Primary School, Romford

# Loneliness

Loneliness is blue, like blue paint,
It sounds like quiet,
It looks very sad,
It feels like your heart is broken,
It smells of nothing,
It tastes like your mouth is full of saltwater,
Actually it reminds me of when my grandma died.

**Holly Peck (7)**
St Edward's CE Primary School, Romford

# My Teacher

Maths lover,
Teddy lover,
Damp hater,
Butterfly chaser,
Home lover,
Bird scarer,
Food eater,
Present lover,
Summer runner,
Snowman maker,
Good listener
And that's
My teacher.

**Temi Abatan (8)**
St Edward's CE Primary School, Romford

# Anger

Anger is red,
Anger is lightning,
Anger is fire,
Anger is spooky,
Anger is cruel.

**Charlie Turner (7)**
St Edward's CE Primary School, Romford

# Happiness

H appiness is yellow and sunny.
A lways makes me feel good.
P erfume, honey and flowers and are what happiness smell like.
P lums, sugar, icing and cake are what happiness tastes of.
I n summer there is lots of happiness.
N ice and soft is the feeling of happiness.
E asy to enjoy like when there's happiness.
S ounds elegant like bells, piano and flute.
S ometimes happiness reminds me of Christmas
  and being with family and friends.

**Hannah Lauder  (10)**
St Edward's CE Primary School, Romford


# Fear

Fear is black, like a stormy night,
It sounds like ghosts going boo,
It looks like bats flying round your head,
It feels like cold hands round your throat,
It tastes like dry sand,
It reminds me of a scary film.

**Lynden Reed  (7)**
St Edward's CE Primary School, Romford


# Love

Love is red like roses that smell so nice each day,
It sounds like people enjoying a lovely holiday,
It looks like children skipping on a nice summer's day,
It feels like people hugging me every day,
It tastes like lovely cold ice cream,
It reminds me of my nice birthday.

**Beth Lamb  (7)**
St Edward's CE Primary School, Romford

# Happiness

Happiness is yellow like sunshine,
It looks like the sun coming down to dance with me,
It smells like yellow daffodils,
It feels like my friends.

**Aiden Jackson  (8)**
**St Edward's CE Primary School, Romford**


# Love

Love is red, like swaying hearts,
It sounds like roses with red hearts,
It looks like swaying hearts in the breeze,
It feels like hearts hugging you squeezed,
It reminds me of hugs.

**Alexandra Wilding  (7)**
**St Edward's CE Primary School, Romford**


# Love

Love is pink, like a pink teddy bear,
It sounds like lovely singing,
It looks like someone playing a harp,
It feels like hot sun and a hot chocolate,
It tastes like a big fire going into your mouth,
It smells like passion fruit,
It reminds me of a pink heart.

**Sian Smith  (7)**
**St Edward's CE Primary School, Romford**

# Love

Love is red, like my heart,
It sounds like water rushing down a hill,
It looks like a sunset that goes down every day,
It feels like a soft lovely bear,
It tastes like a lovely cup of coffee or tea,
It reminds me of the Lord who spreads all his love.

**Abigail Morgan (8)**
**St Edward's CE Primary School, Romford**


# Anger

Anger is black, like a storm cloud,
It feels like a volcano about to erupt,
It sounds like a roller coaster screeching to a halt,
It looks like a horrible monster,
It tastes like a burnt pan of scrambled eggs,
It smells like a horrible mass of ashes,
It reminds me of God's strongest powers.

**Megan Togwell (7)**
**St Edward's CE Primary School, Romford**


# Dopiness

Dopiness is dopey, grey like Eeyore,
It sounds like lightning,
It tastes like fizzy water,
It looks like leaves falling,
It feels like snow,
It reminds me of Eeyore.

**Ashleigh Doman (7)**
**St Edward's CE Primary School, Romford**

# Hate

Hate is red, like fire,
It sounds like thunder and lightning,
It looks like lightning clouds,
It feels like an electric shock,
It tastes like hot, hot flames,
It reminds me of anger and fear.

**Thomas Steer  (7)**
**St Edward's CE Primary School, Romford**

# Romance

Romance is red, like love,
It sounds like fluttering eyelashes,
It looks like red lipstick lip prints,
It smells like ripe strawberries,
It tastes like red wine,
It feels like sweet love,
It reminds me of love.

**Naomi Barwick  (8)**
**St Edward's CE Primary School, Romford**

# Love

Love is white, like a bunny rabbit
Hopping in the meadow.
Love feels like lots of hugs.
Love looks like a butterfly.
Love smells like flowers' pollen.
Love tastes like strawberries and cream.

**Hannah Sayers  (7)**
**St Edward's CE Primary School, Romford**

# Hate

Hate is like anger and being mean,
Its colour is black,
Sounds like dinosaurs in the sky,
Looks like danger,
It smells like steam and smoke,
It feels like being slapped around the face,
It tastes like food you don't like.

**Rachel Phelan  (7)**
St Edward's CE Primary School, Romford

# Darkness

Darkness is black, like a wolf's mouth.
Darkness looks like a big bad wolf.
Darkness sounds like a wolf howling in the wind.
Darkness smells like a bad skunk.
Darkness tastes like the wolf is eating someone.
Darkness feels like the wolf is waiting on the hill for me.
Darkness reminds me of stars in the sky.

**Madeleine Weekes  (7)**
St Edward's CE Primary School, Romford

# Happiness

Happiness is yellow, like the sun in the sky.
Happiness is like music in my head.
It tastes like silence,
It feels warm like a fire,
It looks like the sun.

**Luke Sheridan  (7)**
St Edward's CE Primary School, Romford

# Darkness

Darkness is like a charging night,
Anger is like a red rose,
It sounds like a dark stream.
Fear is like a shaking rattlesnake
But happiness is like a fish swimming in the sea.
It smells like fish, like meat,
The smell flying in the air.

**Nathan Jackson (8)**
St Edward's CE Primary School, Romford

# Love

Love is pink, like a lovely big flower.
Love sounds like the rustling of a tree.
Love tastes like my favourite dinner.
Love smells like a flower's pollen.
Love feels like a warm bath.
Love looks like a beautiful butterfly,
Love reminds me of my lovely family.

**Oliver Portway (7)**
St Edward's CE Primary School, Romford

# Love

Love is white, like a soaring dove,
It sounds like fluttering birds,
It tastes like sweet honey,
It smells like lovely flowers,
It feels like smooth silk,
It looks like a beautiful sunset,
It reminds me of Freckles the fish.

**Nathan Smith (8)**
**St Edward's CE Primary School, Romford**

# Fun

Fun is purple, like a purple flower,
It sounds like the wind blowing it from side to side,
It feels like a funfair,
It looks like lots of birds singing together,
It tastes like sweets,
It smells like sharing,
It reminds me of when I went to St Peter's fair.

**Naomi Vallance (7)**
**St Edward's CE Primary School, Romford**

# Love

Love is red, like a lovebird,
It sounds like birds kissing,
It tastes like juicy apples,
It feels like little rabbits dancing,
It looks like love hearts,
It smells like perfume,
It reminds me of the infants' school.

**Charlotte Neale (7)**
**St Edward's CE Primary School, Romford**

# Love

Love is red, like a ripe apple,
It sounds like someone whistling,
It feels like a fluffy rabbit,
It looks like someone singing,
It tastes like strawberries and ice cream,
It smells like a lemon cake,
It reminds me of my grandads dying.

**Victoria Christmas (7)**
St Edward's CE Primary School, Romford

# Happiness

Happiness is bright yellow, like golden sunshine shining on me,
It sounds like a bird singing sweetly in my head,
It tastes like sweet candy,
It looks like a beautiful day,
It feels like a hot summer holiday,
It smells like sweet plums and sweet grapes,
It reminds me of my first birthday.

**Hannah King (8)**
St Edward's CE Primary School, Romford

# Love

Love is red, like a nice juicy heart,
It sounds like a whispering white flower,
It tastes like a bright golden apple.
Love looks like the scent of rivers flowing.
Love feels like fat juicy candyfloss,
It reminds me of pink fluffy rabbits.

**Karen Morris (7)**
St Edward's CE Primary School, Romford

# Happiness

Happiness is a bright yellow, sunny afternoon,
It sounds like a soaring dove in the sky,
It feels like a warm evening,
It looks like a wonderful day,
It tastes like sweet honey,
It smells like beautiful flowers,
It reminds me of my first birthday.

**Jade Hill  (8)**
**St Edward's CE Primary School, Romford**


# Happiness

Happiness is yellow, like a bright sun in the sky.
Happiness sounds like birds flying in the sky.
Happiness feels like picking up a sunflower.
Happiness looks like a fish swimming in the sea.
Happiness tastes like a big banana.
Happiness smells like strong, bright perfume.
Happiness reminds me of when I first saw my nan in Spain.

**Rosie Webber  (7)**
**St Edward's CE Primary School, Romford**


# Anger

Anger is red, like a fierce, exploding volcano,
It feels like rough bark,
It smells like burnt food,
It tastes like rotten apples,
It looks like fire raging in a building.

**Samuel Gowland  (7)**
**St Edward's CE Primary School, Romford**

# Fun

Fun is yellow, like the sun.
Fun tastes like peaches.
Fun is like music in your head.
Fun reminds me of the day
We had Jeans for Genes Day.
Thank you Lord for laughter
And for fun.

**Fraser Clark (7)**
St Edward's CE Primary School, Romford

# Love

Love is red, like a rose.
Love sounds like romantic music.
Love smells like calm water.
Love feels like flowers in the wind.
Love looks like a lovely red heart.
Love tastes like a lovely heart,
It reminds me of my heart.

**Chloe Hammond (7)**
St Edward's CE Primary School, Romford

# Fear

F is for frightened when there is a war.
E is for the emotions when you have fear.
A is the colour of amber when you don't feel ready.
R tastes like rhubarb, very sour.

**Elizabeth McDonald (9)**
St Edward's CE Primary School, Romford

# Happiness

H is for hippo, an animal that God made.
A is for apple, a fruit that grows on trees.
P is for pineapple that is really juicy.
P is for pig that snorts really loudly.
I is for innocent that we say we are.
N is for nice like a colourful rolling dice.
E is for egg like a non-oval peg.
S is for sugar so sweet but not sour.
S is for slide, chopping wheat and corn to the side.

**Ebenezer Oluwole (9)**
St Edward's CE Primary School, Romford

# Love

L is for love, one of the most important things in life.
O is for orange the colour of love.
V is for Valentine because Valentine is all about love.
E is for evidence of love.

**Sophie Doyle (9)**
St Edward's CE Primary School, Romford

# Love

Love is bright,
Love is white,
Love is on Earth,
Love is for marriage,
Love is a step forward
And love is everyone.

**Ryan McNamara**
St Edward's CE Primary School, Romford

# Love

Love is the colour of red, like a rose that blows in the wind.
Love sounds like a kind and caring person.
Love tastes like a sweet.
Love smells like a beautiful flower.
Love feels like a warm, fluffy pillow.
Love reminds me of the people I love.

**Daisy Harper  (9)**
**St Edward's CE Primary School, Romford**


# Anger

Anger is black.
Anger sounds like *grrrr!*
Anger tastes like egg.
Anger smells like fear.
Anger feels like sadness.

**Albert Parnell  (9)**
**St Edward's CE Primary School, Romford**


# Fear

Fear is a dull colour,
It sounds creepy.
Fear tastes rotten,
It smells like danger,
It feels tingly,
It reminds me of scary things.

**Michael Stannard  (9)**
**St Edward's CE Primary School, Romford**

# Happiness

H appiness is a beautiful colour of bright yellow like the sun
A nd tiny stars are twinkling at the beautiful sound of it.
P eople love the taste of it though because it tastes very sweet!
P eople also love the smell because it smells like gorgeous flowers,
I think happiness feels like a really small, smooth, round pebble.
N ice things bring lots and lots of happiness!
E veryone enjoys being happy because it's wonderful!
S haring also brings lots of happiness.
S miling at each other makes lots of people very happy!

Happiness makes me feel really warm and glowing inside!
It's a great emotion!

**Emma Cottrell (9)**
St Edward's CE Primary School, Romford


# Hate

Hate is as red as blood,
It sounds like shouting,
It tastes bitter and sour,
It feels very rough
And it smells like a tip.

**Abigail Howson (9)**
St Edward's CE Primary School, Romford


# My Hamster Harry

My hamster Harry is the bounciest
hamster in the world,
he bounces from place to place
and he even bounces on the chair.

**Jaron Escoffery (8)**
St Edward's CE Primary School, Romford

# Happiness

H is for happiness.
A is for about the way you feel about it like it feels like you will always be happy forever.
P is for purple.
P is for perfect.
I is for I like the smell because it smells of sweet flowers.
N is for nice and sweet.
E is for each thing that is nice has a nice meaning.
S is for smiley faces.
S is for singing people.

**Rachel Stewart (9)**
**St Edward's CE Primary School, Romford**


# Love

Love is pink and nice and warm,
Love is the sound of a bird singing,
Love tastes like chocolate melting in my mouth,
Love smells like red, red roses,
Love feels soft and cuddly,
Love reminds me of beautiful flowers.

**Rianna Veares (9)**
**St Edward's CE Primary School, Romford**


# Hate

Hate tastes likes a sour lollipop.
Hate is a very strong word.
Hate is browny-black like a mouldy apple core.
Hate smells like gone-off milk.
Hate feels like a volcano has just erupted in your heart.

**Rowanne Simpson (9)**
**St Edward's CE Primary School, Romford**

# Love

Love is the colour of red, like a heart,
It sounds like someone loving a hot bath,
It tastes like sweets rumbling in my tummy,
It smells like roses in the cold autumn,
It feels so soft like a cuddly teddy.
Love was what I was talking about
And it reminds me of my mummy.

**Antony Dashfield (9)**
**St Edward's CE Primary School, Romford**


# I Wish, I Wish

I wish I had a fish on a little dish,
That is what I wish, I wish.

I wish I had a shark and a big, big park
And that is what I wish, I wish.

But I wish the most for friends and family
And that is what I wish, I wish.

**Deanna Newstead**
**St Edward's CE Primary School, Romford**


# The Cane

'Aah, reminds me of the old days,' said the teacher.
The cheekiest girl walked up to the teacher and said,
'Go on Sir.'
'OK just a tap.'
'Are you sure?'
'Yep.'

**Samuel Cockburn (8)**
**St Edward's CE Primary School, Romford**

# You

Roses are red, violets blue,
Your head belongs to the zoo.

Roses are red, violets are black,
Do me a favour and sit on a tack.

Roses are red, violets are blue,
You smell of flowers in forest that grew.

**Daniella Anderson (8)**
St Edward's CE Primary School, Romford

# Seaside

S is for sun that shines in the sky.
E is for excited children.
A is for afternoon when grown-ups walk on the sand.
S is for sand that is nice and gold.
I is for ice cream that is running down the cone.
D is for disgusting seaweed in the water.
E is for everyone having fun.

**Olajoke Olaniyan (8)**
St Edward's CE Primary School, Romford

# Ollie

Ollie, Ollie, Ollie he lived in a trolley,
Everyone pushed him around,
But he said, 'Where am i going?
Everyone pushes me around.'
But Ollie you live in a trolley,
So you can't help that you are one.

**Alice Pugh (8)**
St Edward's CE Primary School, Romford

# I Wish I Could Fly

My younger brother blew up a balloon,
Went in the garden,
The wind was strong too,
So he blew away frightened and scared.

Then he blew in a tree,
Jumped down with glee,
Landed with a bee, didn't say a word,
My family came out in a herd and said,
*Not me.*

So he went upstairs silly and felt like dead,
Went back downstairs dizzy and frizzy,
And then went outside jumped so high,
*Don't do that again.*

**Max Lagrossi (8)**
**St Edward's CE Primary School, Romford**


# Black Bats

Wow! Look at that,
A great big bat.
There are tens of thousands,
What are thousands?
For there's much more than we can count,
They're black,
They're bold,
They've even got mould,
They live in caves,
What are caves?
They've got pointy ears
And tiny feet
And slimy little eyes.

**Sophie Hughes (8)**
**St Edward's CE Primary School, Romford**

# Mouse Fun

There is a mouse
In his house,
He is singing to his friends
A song that never ever ends.

He sings on and on
Till he's twenty-one.

He sings in the summer sun,
He sings in the winter moon,
He sings in the autumn in the afternoon,
He sings in the spring when he's happy and sad.

He sings in the morning when the day is begun,
He sings on the beach chewing chewing gum,
He sings everywhere and every day,
He likes to sing day to day.

He carries on singing till he's forty-two,
We know he's singing just for you!

**Emma Hatwell  (8)**
St Edward's CE Primary School, Romford


# The Feel Of Anger

Anger makes you feel hot red, fierce
And as if you are going to explode.
Anger feels like you are going to charge,
Running really fast.
Anger leaves a sour taste
And you may become bitter.
Anger is the smell of a volcano
Exploding out hot boiling lava.

**Claire Jackson  (9)**
St Edward's CE Primary School, Romford

# The Fish Who Made A Wish

I once had a fish
Who made a wish,
To be a knight
Scared of the light.
So he crept out at dark
And gave a quick bark.
Then the sun rose up,
They said, 'Now he's in luck,'
And tucked himself away.
Then one day,
Someone took him away
And was never seen again.

**Misha Goddard  (8)**
St Edward's CE Primary School, Romford


# The Funny Mouse

One day a little mouse
Came to my nest.
It said to me, 'I've found a bee.'
'Oh no,' said I, 'I must fly.'

**Sarah Brown  (8)**
St Edward's CE Primary School, Romford


# Football

Football is fun, you can kick it all around,
You can kick it on the ground and header it down.
You can jump up high, you can run fast,
Pass to your players and score a goal.
Yes West Ham you're the crown of the down.

**Rachel Podd  (8)**
St Edward's CE Primary School, Romford

# A Girl Came Home

A girl came home
And she only moaned.

She moaned at my dad,
She moaned at my lad,
She moaned at my mum.

She moaned in the kitchen,
She moaned in the hallway
And she moaned away.

**Sophie Bowtell (8)**
**St Edward's CE Primary School, Romford**


## I Don't Get My Way

I never ever get my way,
I stay in bed all day.
Even when visitors come
I never ever get to play
Because I always eat my gum
They still never ever say I'm fun!

**Raelle Pickton (8)**
**St Edward's CE Primary School, Romford**


# Happiness

Happiness is bright yellow and glows all around,
It glitters and sparkles and is easily found,
In a touch from friends' hands,
Or the care of someone who understands,
In the hearing of laughter
And the joy that stays after,
In the smell of cakes baking,
Happiness is much sweeter - and is yours for the taking.

**Élise Herring (9)**
**St Edward's CE Primary School, Romford**

# Football

Football is the best,
It comes from the west
And if you come from the west
You get the best.

Football is the best,
It comes from a man called the best
And if you hear the best
You are the best.

Football is the best,
It comes from the best
And if you hear best
Football is the best.

Football is the best
It comes from the best
And if you are the best
You are wrong because football is the best.

God is the best
He made football the best
And if you are the best
Football is the best.

God is the best
He is the best
And when you think football is the best
You are right, football is the *best*.

**Jack Hull  (8)**
**St Edward's CE Primary School, Romford**

# Anger

Anger is red, like hot peppers in your head,
It reminds me of the time when my sister
Blew up like a big balloon.

**Abbie Legallienne  (8)**
**St Edward's CE Primary School, Romford**

# My Teacher Is Cool

My teacher is the coolest,
She should be in a book
For she is the coolest in the room,
Should she not,
Her book would be called.
Some teachers are cool
And guess what?
She grew very tall,
Then she grew very small,
Then she wasn't cool at all.

**Jessica Stone  (9)**
St Edward's CE Primary School, Romford


# My Cat

My cat is fat, it eats my hats,
It's so horrible to see.
It tries to eat our feet
And I don't like the feel.
It doesn't like to be alone,
But it does not have a mobile phone.
He doesn't have a juicy bone
But it was alone.

**Emma Aston  (8)**
St Edward's CE Primary School, Romford


# Anger

Anger is like a volcano with its lava spilling out.
Anger is like curry burning your throat.
Anger is red-hot.

**Gemma Willson  (8)**
St Edward's CE Primary School, Romford

# Pets

I have a pet cat called Stitch,
She has caramel-brown, black and white fur,
She is very crazy.
Please keep a secret,
Once she ate a mince pie.

I have a pet cat called Jess,
He is not as mad as Stitch,
But he's the type for me.
He is midnight-black,
For he is the greatest tomboy *ever*,
So he is the type for me.

**Imogen Rayment-Smith  (8)**
**St Edward's CE Primary School, Romford**


# Sport

There's plenty of sports
Like football and pool,
But football's just the best,
Well it's better than the rest.
West Ham yes the best in the world.
West Ham 5 - Chelsea 0.

**Sam Blowers  (9)**
**St Edward's CE Primary School, Romford**


# Sea

There was a fish
Who wanted a dish.
He wished and wished
Till he got a dish,
Until a shark came along
And ate the fish in the dish.

**Alexander Hardy  (8)**
**St Edward's CE Primary School, Romford**

# Football

F ootball is fun and joy,
O h I like to see my team win,
O h I like it when my team is on the pitch,
T ime to play and get the ball,
B oots are good for football,
A ll the time keep your eye on the ball,
L earning is just as good as football,
L earning is hard.

**Christian Wroe (7)**
St Edward's CE Primary School, Romford


# Brownies

B rownies are fun,
R unning and playing games,
O nly an hour to go,
W e have fun playing,
N o we can never give up,
I 'm always on the go,
E very Thursday,
S o see you soon, have a nice afternoon.

**Jessica Pitts (8)**
St Edward's CE Primary School, Romford


# Gymnastics

Gymnastics is fun,
But it hurts your bum.
If I fall off a beam,
I scream.

**Elena Sheridan (8)**
St Edward's CE Primary School, Romford

# Trips

I like going on trips,
My best trips are holidays to Spain or New York.
I go on trains to places or in a car,
Or taking off on a jet plane.

If you walk to the shops or up to bed,
You are on a trip,
To get some bread or to rest your head,
I like trips.

**Katherine Miller (8)**
St Edward's CE Primary School, Romford

# Sport

Sport is fun,
Ice skating is a great sport,
Gliding along the ice,
Rugby is rough,
Although very fun,
Basketball includes a lot of jumping.

**Libby Ryder (8)**
St Edward's CE Primary School, Romford

# Swimming

My trunks are black,
The water is blue,
How I love swimming,
Oh yes I do.

**Michael Nance (8)**
St Edward's CE Primary School, Romford

# Untitled

*Lemons*
Lemons are yellow,
They look all sunny,
But when you eat them
Your tongue goes funny.

*Markets*
Markets are busy,
The skies are blue,
The sun is yellow,
So are you!

**Joel Oyelese  (8)**
**St Edward's CE Primary School, Romford**


# Colours

The sky is blue,
The sun is yellow,
The sand is green,
Chocolate is brown,
Shapes are red,
Dogs are white and black,
Books are orange,
Many colours are around.

**William Borg  (8)**
**St Edward's CE Primary School, Romford**


# Match Of The Day

On Monday I scored a goal,
On Tuesday I did a foul,
On Wednesday I scored a goal.

**Jake Gear  (8)**
**St Edward's CE Primary School, Romford**

# Colours

The sky is blue,
The sun is yellow,
The grass is green,
The wall is brown,
I love colours.

The floor is red,
The page is white,
The table is pink,
The box is orange,
I love colours.

**Siân West (8)**
**St Edward's CE Primary School, Romford**


# Red

Red is the colour of love,
Red is the colour of the Devil,
Red is the colour of sunburn,
Red is the colour of fire,
Red is the colour of anger.

**Pollyanna Clark (9)**
**St Edward's CE Primary School, Romford**


# School, School, School

School, school, school,
Always working.
School, school, school,
Playtime's the best.
School, school, school.

**Lucy Andrean (8)**
**St Edward's CE Primary School, Romford**

# Butterflies, Butterflies

Butterflies, butterflies
All red and blue,
They come in different colours too.
Every day you see them fluttering around
And if you're lucky they might land on the ground.
Butterflies, butterflies they're so nice to see
Them fluttering around and they like you and me.
I love butterflies, they're sweet and soft
And sometimes you may get them in your loft.

**Lauren Angus-Larkin (8)**
St Edward's CE Primary School, Romford


# Butterflies And Friends

The butterflies are in their trees
Talking to the birds that sing
And the mice are downstairs nibbling their cheese.
The crocodile is washing clothes
And the frog's on his lily pad.
The elephant's proud of his trunk
And the lion is hiding in his mane.

**Alexandra Wood (8)**
St Edward's CE Primary School, Romford


# Teacher, Teacher

'Teacher, teacher, I've lost my book.'
'Well you will have to look,' said the teacher.
'Teacher, teacher you're so unfair,
So much you will have to go to Mr Blair.
Teacher, teacher you always shout,
So much you chuck us out.'

**George Goldrick (8)**
St Edward's CE Primary School, Romford

# My Blades

My blades flash
With a bump
And a bash.
I love to skate
Although I'm always late,
I love to win
And throw the others in the bin.
I love skating, it's my thing,
So I will skate all day
And I'll skate all night.

**Jessica-Rose Spong  (8)**
St Edward's CE Primary School, Romford


# George The Great

George the Great is so great
He can even climb school walls,
And he also has great powers
So he can save all the people
In the school if there is a fire.

**Hope Garnish  (8)**
St Edward's CE Primary School, Romford


# Marvellous Michael

Michael Owen is in this poem,
So be careful what you read,
Football, football everywhere, now 24 good deeds.

Everyone knows Michael's the best,
If you like Beckham, give it a rest.

Michael plays like one of a kind,
If you support Michael, I wouldn't mind!

**Anna Bradford  (10)**
St George's RC Primary School, Southend-on-Sea

# Herbie The Tortoise

Herbie is a very fast runner,
Even though he doesn't have a mother,
Caroline looks after him a lot,
I'm scared he might just go kerplot.

His food is just dead leaves and flowers,
He eats them like he has super powers,
People think he'll be soon dead,
But I think he'll grow instead.

I don't think Herbie will ever die,
If he does I'll be surprised,
Herbie is so strong and healthy,
I bet he wishes to be free.

Herbie is the best,
He's better than the rest.

**Kaleigh Holley (10)**
**St George's RC Primary School, Southend-on-Sea**


# Betty Brown

Betty Brown bought a balloon
But it burst.
So Betty Brown bought a bouncy ball
But it popped.
So Betty Brown bought a book
But it tore.
So Betty Brown bawled her eyes out
But she blew up.
That was the end of Betty Brown.

**Rhiannon Tyrie (11)**
**St George's RC Primary School, Southend-on-Sea**

# Spurs

T he best in the Prem',
O verall I love them,
T hey are the best,
T hey never rest,
E very day they train,
N ever-ending reign,
H ome and away
A lways we pray,
*M erciless!*

R unning till 90 minutes,
O utwitting and no sins,
C ome on you Spurs,
K arate moves occur.

T hey always pass the test,
H ome and away we are the best,
*E asy!*

P erfect at our game,
R ampaging Defoe is our main,
E verybody on this land,
M an Henry is in the sand,
 I hate Man U,
E asy thing to do,
R ight up the top,
S purs never stop,
H alting we never do,
 I love them oh yes I do,
*P erfect!*

M an we rule,
A rsenal drool,
*N atural!*

**Jared Brand (10)**
**St George's RC Primary School, Southend-on-Sea**

# Football

F ans coming from everywhere to support their team,
O fficial merchandise from every team,
O nly the best the fans want,
T he match is 90 minutes long,
B efore matches they are feeling excited,
A way matches are worse,
L eaving after the match feeling happy or sad,
L etting your feelings out.

I t is the best sport ever,
S pying on the opposite team.

T he best team normally wins,
H ome matches are better,
E veryone wants their team to win.

B est feeling is winning a cup,
E veryone cheering for their team,
S taying at the top of the table,
T urning up to support their team.

S potting your favourites,
P ointing to them
O ver people's heads,
R unning with them,
T rying to spot them.

E very player feeling hot,
V ery skilful they are,
E veryone feeling tired,
R unning on a pitch.

M agical,
A mazing,
D azzling,
E nding the fun happily or sadly.

**Jenny Doherty  (10)**
**St George's RC Primary School, Southend-on-Sea**

# Rage

Rage is something in everyone,
It lays dormant until woken,
It is inside you.

Many think it is something that can be tamed,
But they are wrong,
Rage is wild.

One in a million,
Never gets infected,
Rage is poison.

Rage can haunt you
Until you die,
Rage is a curse.

Rage has many enemies
All around,
Rage has no mercy.

**Natasha Woodward (11)**
St George's RC Primary School, Southend-on-Sea


# War

War, war very dangerous,
Bullets being fired, murdering innocent bodies.
War, war very dangerous,
People bombing many cities full of innocent people.
War, war very dangerous,
Innocent men being forced to fight in foreign lands.
War, war very dangerous,
As people throw their lives away:
War, war an awful thing.

**George Gillett (10)**
St George's RC Primary School, Southend-on-Sea

# Desert

In the heart of the hot Arizona Desert
Where only lizards and snakes dwell
You'd sell your soul for water,
In the Arizona Desert.

Surrounded by rocks and sand,
Vultures and eagles circling above,
Animal bones scattered on the ground,
In the Arizona Desert.

On the horizon you see a city
Through the light, clear blue sky
And you hope you make it to the end,
In the Arizona Desert.

**Alexander Leighton (10)**
**St George's RC Primary School, Southend-on-Sea**

# Dragons

Dragons steal your finest sheep and cows,
Maybe the odd child or two.

If anyone comes near the flesh-eating
Dragon's lair all will fear its peril,
Blood, flesh and life gone in a second,
All bones are chucked in a poor villager's house,
Can no one save us, anyone?

On a fine summer's day a boy comes with help
Nor rich, nor strong just a scruffy boy like a tramp,
In an instant a raging fire spouts,
Out comes the boy with nothing but a burnt foot
Limping with the head of the flesh-eating dragon.

**Savannah Lawrence (10)**
**St George's RC Primary School, Southend-on-Sea**

# My Dream

The dream I had is the one
That will stick with me.

The place I thought about was magical
Where there was only the fresh green grass
And the fields which have rainbows crossing over them.

There were no guns or wars,
Only kind people who share
And give generously.

Where you know day
And night you'd be safe to go
Outside and play.

A good life with your friends
And family so that is my dream.

What about yours?

**Liam Clark (10)**
**St George's RC Primary School, Southend-on-Sea**


# Footie

Tennis, nah,
Golf, OK,
Footie, yeah,
Footie is great wherever you play.
It's the best game in the world.
The rest of the sports are never good
But footie is the best.
The players in Arsenal mostly play well but I don't care.
Footie is *great!*

**Michael Irlam (10)**
**St George's RC Primary School, Southend-on-Sea**

# Schooldays

My friends are really nice to me,
They normally invite me round for tea.
They cheer me up when I am down,
They hardly ever make me frown.
My friends are cheerful, every one,
So come on in and join the fun.

My friends don't just hang with me,
Sometimes we hang in a three.
Lunch is always our best place,
Maggie our cook, has a cheerful face.
Dinner ladies help with all that needs done,
If you get on their right side they're really fun.

Break is our first burst of air,
Only 15 minutes, do you think it's fair?
When we're in it's time to work,
Some people really act a jerk.
Mrs Welsby isn't all that strict,
Be nice, for as our teacher she was picked.

We're meant to be quiet while we are busy,
We sometimes play buzz fizzy.
Friends are always here to see,
The boys just have to flick a pea.
Games is active and cool,
Most play football.

Lunch is an hour and a half,
But we still have a laugh.
After hot dinners,
We all are winners.
So that was what it's like at school,
Now you know it's not that cool.

**Hannah Wallen (10)**
**St George's RC Primary School, Southend-on-Sea**

## My Riddle

I have lots of legs
And I bend and curl,
And I can swirl.
I can crawl up stems
And I eat leaves.
You often find me on trees.
What am I?

Caterpillar.

I have two legs,
I wear shoes,
I can run, jump, hop and skip,
I often go to school,
What am I?

Me.

**Hannah Hoswell (10)**
St George's RC Primary School, Southend-on-Sea

## Fat Fred

Fat Fred is sooo fat,
He's always hungry,
He once ate our welcome mat.
Fat Fred is sooo dim,
He's never been clever,
He once went for a swim
In piranha-ridden water,
That was the end of him.

**Thomas Sharland-Harris (10)**
St George's RC Primary School, Southend-on-Sea

# Magpies

Magpies fly high,
Magpies fly low,
I think it's a shame when they go.

When they sing it's nice to hear,
They call at me when I'm near.

Magpies come in pairs,
I think they're nicer than eclairs.

Magpies are black and white,
If they weren't here it wouldn't be right.

**Emma Callowhill (10)**
**St George's RC Primary School, Southend-on-Sea**


# My Best Friend

My best friend is Paul,
He likes playing football,
He doesn't care
If there is no one there.

My best friend is Paul,
He goes for a paddle in the pool.
He swims here and there,
Having fun.

My best friends is Paul,
He is as fast as fast can be,
He dodges here and there.

**Colm Coughlan (10)**
**St George's RC Primary School, Southend-on-Sea**

# My Brother

My brother is fat, my brother is thin,
I don't really care about the colour of the skin.
He looks so cute but he isn't at all,
'Cause last night he burst a great big beach ball.
Just think a little while later,
Look at the time,
We'll just be playing and it'll be just fine.

**Paul Johnson  (10)**
St George's RC Primary School, Southend-on-Sea


# My Best Friend - Haiku

My best fri~ ~d Colm
He thinks I am fantastic
But he's elastic.

**Roman Gabrielczyk  (10)**
St George's RC Primary School, Southend-on-Sea


# My Best Friend Tortoise

He's small and he's soft,
He lives in the loft,
He eats lettuce and leaves,
He'll chew on your sleeves,
He stays in a tank
And sits on the bank,
He stays there all night
And in the morning he'll bite,
On his lettuce and leaves.

**Robert Palmer  (10)**
St George's RC Primary School, Southend-on-Sea

# Horses

People ride horses in the saddle,
Horses like trotting in the muddy puddles,
Horses ride fast at the races,
They set themselves at the right pace.
Horses, horses in the field,
Playing nicely they should never be killed.

**Caroline Sharman (11)**
St George's RC Primary School, Southend-on-Sea

# Limerick

There was an old lady from Surrey
Who ate hot vindaloos and curry,
One day she fell ill
Whilst taking a pill,
P'raps it was all that hot curry.

**Emily Skipp (10)**
St Peter's CE Primary School, Sible Hedingham

# Monkeys

I like monkeys, they're so sweet,
They swing in trees and like to leap.
Some live in zoos, some are free,
Some of them love swinging in trees.

They're brown and furry and lots of fun,
They also like to lay in the sun.
They play hide-and-seek in a bush or a tree,
But they are most of all happy when they are free.

**Pippa Sharp (8)**
St Peter's CE Primary School, Sible Hedingham

# A Magician's Lair

Inside this creepy cave
Lives a magician called Dave.
All of his potions
And silly commotions,
He keeps this secret from all,
Even though there are eyes on the wall.
I've heard his latest spell
Is to turn a duck into a bell.
Unfortunately the duck is wise,
And no matter how hard he tries,
The duck will always get away,
So he'll have to try another day.

**Danielle Rainer (9)**
**St Peter's CE Primary School, Sible Hedingham**


# Fish Poem

Once there was a fish,
That sat on a dish,
Wiggling its tail and being sick.
Then he met a goldfish,
But he wasn't being sick.
Then he ate fish food,
But it didn't taste that good,
So they jumped out of the bowl,
And ate all the food in the fridge.
Then they fell down a ditch,
And they haven't eaten for ages.

**Jade Cook (9)**
**St Peter's CE Primary School, Sible Hedingham**

# It's Hallowe'en tonight

If you want to be scared tonight
This is where you should be

In the town at night knocking on people's doors
And saying, 'Trick or treat'

Ghosts and bats
Giving you a fright

You need to go out
Because it's Hallowe'en tonight.

**Zoe Lee (9)**
**St Peter's CE Primary School, Sible Hedingham**


# Hallowe'en

If you want a fright
Be about tonight

Bugs and itches
Devils and witches
Cut-out pumpkins

Orange munchkins
Skeletons and wolves

People being fools
Lots of sweets
In for some treats.

**Lucy Edwards (9)**
**St Peter's CE Primary School, Sible Hedingham**

# My Guinea Pigs

I love my guinea pigs,
They are cute, cuddly and sweet,
What a lazy life they have,
They just sleep, nibble and eat.

They live in a hutch,
Which is kept in the shed,
With food, water and hay in it,
Gives them a cosy bed.

When it turns warm outside,
They spend all day in their run,
Nibbling at the grass and weeds,
And relaxing in the sun.

**Harriet Tame (10)**
**St Peter's CE Primary School, Sible Hedingham**


# Thief

I am a thief,
I have no teeth,
I'm always very cold,
But then I'm very old.
Next year I hope to turn a new leaf.
My sister has loads of friends
And I steal her hens.
I see a mouse,
Everybody get in your house.
Guess my name!
My name is Jim
And I'm very slim.

**Callum Silverback-Radford (9)**
**St Peter's CE Primary School, Sible Hedingham**

# Up In The Attic

Old rusty key
Very cold
Miniature doll
A picture of me
My old coat
A Christmas tree
A pile of old clothes
I made that model goat
Box of books
A toy yacht boat
Crisp boxes
Old dusty coat
Up in the attic.

**Lucy Everitt (10)**
St Peter's CE Primary School, Sible Hedingham


# Winters

W inter is here and we are all having fun
I gloos made on the ground
N o more school
T rees all icy in the snow
E veryone is getting a cold
R aindrops falling on the ground
S nowball fights in the cold
  *No more wasps, yeah!*

**Sydney Hunter (8)**
St Peter's CE Primary School, Sible Hedingham


# Humpty Dumpty

Humpty Dumpty sat on the wall eating black bananas,
A cow fell down and broke his crown,
So he had to go to the doctor's
To have some sultanas.

**Natalie Purcell (9)**
St Peter's CE Primary School, Sible Hedingham

# Horrible Habits

A is for Abby who makes lots of noise
B is for Bethany who bullies the boys
C is for Chanelle who teases the cat
D is for Dexter whose singing is flat
E is for Emily who's never on time
F is for Frank who's covered in slime
G is for Gemma who never says thanks
H is for Harlie who plans to rob banks
I is for Kian who slams the door
J is for Jade whose jokes are a bore
K is for Karen who won't wash her face
L is for Lucy who cheats in a race
M is for Maisy who gobbles her food
N is for Nicola who runs about in the nude
O is for Ollie who treads on your toes
P is for Peter who will pick his nose
Q is for Queenie who won't tell the truth
R is for Robert who's very uncouth
S is for Sam who bellows and bawls
T is for Tom who scribbles on walls
U is for Una who fidgets too much
V is for Victoria who talks double Dutch
W is for Wilma who won't wipe her feet
X is for Xerxes who never is neat
Y is for Yorick who is vain as can be and
Z is for Zoe who doesn't love me.

**Harlie Cornish  (10)**
**St Peter's CE Primary School, Sible Hedingham**

# Animals

A is for anteater eating lots of ants,
B is for bear eating honey,
C is for camel with his lumpy back,
D is for dolphin jumping in the sea,
E is for elephant with his big ears,
F is for frog hopping around,
G is for giraffe with its long neck,
H is for hedgehog with his spiky back,
I is for ibex with big horns,
J is for jackal roaring like mad,
K is for kangaroo jumping around,
L is for llama spitting at you,
M is for monkey swinging from trees,
N is for nit jumping from head to head,
O is for owl swooping at night,
P is for pig rolling in mud,
Q is for quail flying in the sky,
R is for rhino with his big horn,
S is for sheep all fleecy and woolly,
T is for tortoise with his big shell,
U is for umbrella bird with his pointy feet,
V is for vole hiding away,
W is for whale, the biggest in the sea,
X is for X-ray fish swimming in the sea,
Y is for yak, so big and strong,
Z is for zebra, all stripy.

**Rosie Ranson (9)**
**St Peter's CE Primary School, Sible Hedingham**

# Bonfire Night

Banging and flashing,
Exploding and shouting,
Dashing and whizzing,
Smoking, fading and raging . . .

Dancing and boogying,
Frittering and glittering,
Beeping and eating,
Drinking and sipping . . .

Running and looking,
Crying and wiggling,
Moaning and groaning
And *bang!*

**Bethany Smith (8)**
South Wootton Junior School, King's Lynn


# The Disco

Flashing and dashing,
Dancing and grooving,
Eating and talking,
Playing and getting,
Booming and boogying,
Clapping and shouting,
Twisting and watching,
Jumping and going,
Skipping and enjoying,
Drinking and looking,
Tripping and slipping,
Zooming and running,
All at the disco.

**Scarlett Fountain (8)**
South Wootton Junior School, King's Lynn

# My House

Booming and moaning and shouting and groaning,
Boiling and cooking and chatting and running.
Banging and barking and growling and throwing,
Playing and rushing and falling and dashing.

Thrashing and building and washing and munching,
Clashing and raging and eating and crunching,
Pouring and jumping and begging and sizzling.

Kicking and hitting and smacking and rolling,
Slapping and clapping and flapping and flying,
Writing and rubbing and baking and breaking,
Slurping and tripping and chewing and roaring.

Counting and dropping and drinking a cup of tea,
Bouncing and working and watching and driving,
Making and pulling and pushing and laughing,
What a noisy place!

**Kasey Cannon  (8)**
**South Wootton Junior School, King's Lynn**


# The Swimming Pool

Swimming and diving,
Splashing and clashing,
Showering and washing,
Having fun in the pool,
Backstroking and front-crawling,
And jumping and bubbling,
Laughing and yelling,
And running and walking,
Whistling and shivering,
And playing and watching,
Playing and queuing,
Having fun in the pool!

**Holly Young  (8)**
**South Wootton Junior School, King's Lynn**

# In The Kitchen

Bubbling of the saucepan,
Ticking of the clock,
Mumbling of the kettle and
Sizzling of the wok,
Dripping of the tap,
Gurgling of the drain,
Popping of the pan and
Children munching their tea!

**Madeleine Massingham  (8)**
**South Wootton Junior School, King's Lynn**


# Things I Don't Like

*(In the style of Robert Louis Stevenson)*

Whenever my mum says go to bed,
I always pretend I've hurt my head,
But of course I never get way,
And stay in my bed for all the day.

Whenever my mum says, 'Tidy your room.'
I always have to get out my broom,
I sweep away the dirt and mess,
And put away my very best dress.

Whenever my dad says, 'Do your homework.'
I always pretend I'm out with Kirk,
When I get home I don't get away,
And have to do it for the next day.

Whenever my dad says, 'Go to your room.'
I go up in a very nasty fume,
When he calls me down for tea,
I come down and dance with glee.

**Jonathan Harvey  (11)**
**South Wootton Junior School, King's Lynn**

# At The Vet's

I see the animals crashing and dashing,
Flashing and smashing,
Racing and darting,
Spinning and rolling,
Screeching and screaming,
Bumping and thumping,
Slipping and sliding.

I see the vets rushing and dashing,
Pacing and running,
Banging and shrieking,
Clanking and crashing,
Tripping and operating.

I see the owners,
Moaning and groaning,
Waiting and shouting,
Crying and sobbing,
Staying and hesitating,
Adopting and thinking,
And all that happens at the vet's.

**Georgeina Jarman (8)**
South Wootton Junior School, King's Lynn


# At The Seaside

*(In the style of Robert Louis Stevenson)*

When I am standing by the sea
And all the fish are next to me
I jump right in and have a laugh
Then I go home and have a bath
I'll go back to the beach next week
To have the sea back at my feet
I'll run around and jump and play
I wish I went there every day.

**James Cave (10)**
South Wootton Junior School, King's Lynn

# At The Basketball Match

Bouncing and jumping,
Cheering and shouting and shooting and scoring,
Booing and shrieking and drinking and eating,
Pushing and slaving, winning and beating,
Sweating and huffing and puffing,
Turning and barging, swirling and tricking,
Tripping and hurting and twirling around and around.
Wiping and ripping, and whizzing and frizzing,
Flashing and dashing and running.
And whooshing and crashing into each other,
Sticking and liking and sitting and standing,
Watching and slipping and falling and roaring,
And swishing and picking,
Whistling - the end!

**Daniel Cummings (8)**
South Wootton Junior School, King's Lynn


# The Playground

The children were
Shouting and yelling and jumping and bumping,
Running and rushing and gushing and hushing,
Crying and dancing and puffing and huffing,
Thumping and walking and talking,
Making the playground shake!
And hitting and hugging and hopping,
And conkering and smashing,
And falling and shrieking,
And calling and hauling,
And begging and pleading,
And reading and kicking,
And moaning and shivering,
And creeping and peeping.

**Jessica Morgan (8)**
South Wootton Junior School, King's Lynn

# At The Vets

I see the animals leaping and screeching,
And jumping and dashing and moaning,
And groaning and shivering and quivering,
And sweeping and rattling and bumping,
And bouncing and purring,
And barking and running,
And roaring and springing and flapping,
And twisting and whizzing . . .

And creeping and diving,
And flashing and hissing,
And collars on doggies.
And slipping and battling and tripping,
And wagging their tails,
And see the vets rushing and running,
And owners are waiting and sitting,
And rolling and shouting, tiptoeing and stamping,
And kittens are head-butting,
It never stops going . . .
Non-stop listening,
But very good at escaping.

**Emily Ballard  (8)**
**South Wootton Junior School, King's Lynn**


# The Busy Town

Dashing, begging, buying,
Rushing, eating and people shouting,
Moaning, groaning, babies crying . . .

Beeping, ringing and children running,
Queuing, chasing and men waiting.

Pushing and shoving, littering,
Raging and waging, cars parking,
Building, music blaring.
At last we're home!

**Nadine McCrory  (8)**
**South Wootton Junior School, King's Lynn**

# Haiku - Seasons

*Spring*
Flowers start to burst
Birds nest in sheltered bushes
Fresh and bright mornings

*Summer*
Sizzling sun shining
Twittering birds flying past
Scarlet-red blanket

*Autumn*
Dead leaves fall from trees
Conkers lying on the ground
Blustery winds blow.

*Winter*
Shimmering snowflakes
Footprints deep in a snow sheet
Fingers of ice reach.

**Freya Le Serve (10)**
South Wootton Junior School, King's Lynn


# Basketball Match

Bouncing and shouting,
Yelling and throwing,
Dashing and turning,
Groaning and moaning,
Rising and leaping,
Bumping and jumping,
Thundering and twisting,
Whizzing and whacking,
Fouling and clapping and slapping,
Quivering and shivering,
Battling and rattling,
And the bell goes
For the end of the match.

**Mark Britton (8)**
South Wootton Junior School, King's Lynn

# The Jungle

Hooting and flying,
Waking and sleeping,
Killing and living,
Eating and starving,
Running and walking,
Roaring and crawling,
Finding and losing,
Drinking and thirsting,
Howling and yowling,
Growing and growling,
Catching and dropping,
Feeding and taking,
Lying and crying,
Chewing and escaping,
Hiding and gliding,
Scavenging and hunting,
Murdering and hurting,
That's what happens
In the jungle!

**Adnaan Tyabjl (9)**
**South Wootton Junior School, King's Lynn**


# At The Gym

People were
Running, rushing,
Flipping, skipping,
Bouncing and springing,
Dashing, flashing,
Split leaping and toe pointing,
Handstanding and cartwheeling,
Whirling and twirling,
Turning and twisting as the lesson goes on,
Jumping and bumping,
Rolling and somersaulting.

**Ellen Walker (8)**
**South Wootton Junior School, King's Lynn**

# Theme Park

Screaming and shouting,
Whizzing and popping,
Eating and drinking,
Whirling and roaring,
Jumping and diving,
Swirling and hurling,
Whiffing and sniffing,
Twisting and crackling,
Smelling and munching,
Chomping and buying,
Giving and slurping,
Dashing and turning,
Twisting and twirling,
Enjoying and clattering,
Clanging and clashing,
Slamming and clinking,
Plopping and plonking,
Clunking and muttering,
Chatting and clashing,
And all this happens
At a theme park.

**Vishaal Thakrar (8)**
**South Wootton Junior School, King's Lynn**

# The Football Stadium

At the football stadium there's
Singing and whistling and jumping,
And roaring and shouting and
Kissing and chanting and scoring,
And saving and smelling and
Pouring and howling and leaping
And striding and queuing and going,
And that's what's at Highbury.

**Michael Playford (8)**
**South Wootton Junior School, King's Lynn**

# At The Launch Site

Firing and flying,
Shrieking and booming,
Aiming and commanding,
Screaming and whizzing,
And crackling, zigzagging, dashing,
And flashing and rumbling, rocketing
And ticking, sparkling and flicking,
Blasting and fuelling and climbing,
And dazzling and landing, exploring
And seeking, reporting
And discussing, returning home safely!

**Ben Creevy (9)**
**South Wootton Junior School, King's Lynn**


# Forest

Swinging and singing,
Shouting and yelling,
Staring and looking,
Crying and canoeing,
Bumping and dumping,
And jumping and landing,
And slithering,
Biting and crawling
And falling and leaping,
Scratching and eating,
And throwing and clinging,
Itching and shredding,
And chewing and tasting,
Running and bashing,
And clashing and scraping.

**Joseph McLauchlan (8)**
**South Wootton Junior School, King's Lynn**

# Norwich's Win!

People queuing for the match,
Screeching, screaming, shouting,
And clapping, cheering, clashing . . .
And muttering, mumbling,
And singing, booming and laughing.

And kicking the football far away,
Then Norwich scores a goal!
By passing, shooting, scoring
And the goalie kicking out the ball
To one of his football team.

And now it's time for the Mexican wave
Because Norwich has scored another goal!
Now it is 2-0 to Norwich City and they win!

**Brandon Catterall (8)**
South Wootton Junior School, King's Lynn


# The Theme Park

The people were
Screaming and shouting,
And shrieking and running,
And dashing and twirling,
And clashing and hissing,
And cheering and leaping,
And hitting and thundering,
And shivering and turning,
And whizzing and yelling,
And thumping and bumping,
And twisting around and around,
And staring at the roller coasters spinning around,
And curling and skipping and clapping,
And roaring and laughing and drinking,
And spitting and boiling and hiding and flashing.

**Marcelle McDonald-Leslie (8)**
South Wootton Junior School, King's Lynn

# Oberdoggy

*(Based on 'Jabberwocky' by Lewis Carroll)*

'Twas fligig, and the slishey coves
Did shior and fimble in the shabe;
All shimsey were the clorocoves
And the shome paths condade.

'Beware the Obberclog, my son!
The jaws that bite, the claws that catch
Beware the Club Club bird, and shun
The shomious Fudnersnath!'

He took his corpal sword in hand:
Long time the faxome foe he sought -
So rested he by the zum zum tree,
And stood awhile in thought.

And as in kuffish thought he stood,
The Obberclog, with eyes of flame,
Came whiffling through the daygay wood
And murbled as it came!

One, two! One, two! And through and through
The corpal blade went flicker flack!
He left it dead, and with its head
He went golideing back.

'And hast thou slain the Obberclog?
Come to my arms, my deamish boy!
O clabjous day! Ballooh ballay!'
He chortled in his joy.

'Twas fligig, and the slishey coves
Did shior and fimble in the shabe;
All shimsey were the clorocoves
And the shome paths condade.

**Sam Miller (10)**
**South Wootton Junior School, King's Lynn**

# The Crazy Zoo

Shrieking and screeching,
Slipping and sliding,
Flying and trying,
Swimming and screaming,
Feeding and watching,
Blaring and bouncing,
Roaring and ripping,
Moaning and groaning . . .

Complaining and accessing,
Bleeping and barking,
Whizzing and rushing,
Fighting and fussing,
Slithering and sliding,
Thundering and jumping,
Clanging and crashing,
Bashing and mashing,
Thumping and bumping
What a crazy zoo is this?

Opening beehives and slithering snakes,
And people are rushing over the rakes . . .
And eating and drinking, watching . . .
And trying to *live!*

**Arrianne Gagen (9)**
**South Wootton Junior School, King's Lynn**


# The Grapevine

*(In the style of Robert Louis Stevenson)*

At my house there's a grapevine
And it twines up and down,
Up the house and never comes down.
It wiggles and wiggles all the way round.

**Georgia Freeman (10)**
**South Wootton Junior School, King's Lynn**

# At The Theme Park

Flashing and dashing
And whizzing and fizzing,
And shouting and screaming,
And turning and twisting,
And rising and dropping,
And shaking and quaking,
And splashing and sliding
And diving down . . .

And whirling and twirling,
And thumping and bumping,
And shining and twining,
And splashing and clashing,
And pouring and roaring,
And fumbling and flinging,
As the roller coasters drop down,
And slapping and flapping,
And leaping and sinking,
And brisking and swifting,
And darting and zooming,
And eating and drinking,
And slurping and munching,
And queuing and paying,
And talking and wondering,
And laughing and playing,
And all that is going on
In the theme park.

**Zane Lin Tham  (8)**
**South Wootton Junior School, King's Lynn**

# My Game Boy

*(In the style of Robert Louis Stevenson)*

I think my Game Boy is really cool,
I wish I could take it to my school,
I'd hide it deep inside my bag,
But if Mum finds it, I'm in for a nag.

**Matthew Hayward  (10)**
**South Wootton Junior School, King's Lynn**

# Dinosaurs

*(Based on 'Jabberwocky' by Lewis Carroll)*

'Twas filling, and the slimy toads
Did lie and giggle in the wind
All quiet were the animals
And the moon shone brightly.

Beware the dinosaurs, my son!
The jaws that bite, the claws that catch
Beware the hummingbird and shun
The ugliest animal.

He took his shining sword in hand
Long time the scary foe he sought
So rested he by the apple tree
And stood a while in thought.

And as in selfish thought he stood
The dinosaur, with eyes of flame
Came whiffling through the longest wood
And burbled as it came.

One, two! One, two! And through and through
The shining blade went snicker-snack
He left it dead and with its head
He went galloping back.

'And have thou slain the dinosaur?
Come to my arms my gallant boy!
Oh fabulous day! Hip hip hooray!'
He chortled in his joy.

'Twas filling, and the slimy toads
Did lie and giggle in the wind
All quiet were the animals
And the moon shone brightly.

**Natalie Panks  (10)**
**South Wootton Junior School, King's Lynn**

# At The Zoo

Monkeys swinging through the trees
Waving to the silvery bees,
Giraffes' necks are very long,
They are twisted and so strong.
Rhinos' horns are very sharp,
They could be used to play the harp.
Dolphins swimming in the deep blue sea
Not having to pay a nasty fee.
Parrots chirping through the vines,
Flashing colour in every sign.
Zebras' stripes cola-black,
Distinctively seen along their back.
Lions' manes are very shaggy,
Their tails are long and baggy.
Tigers' orange bodies bright,
Their fierce skills are quite a sight.
Bears are growly creatures,
They have some angry features.
Penguins are skilful,
They twist and dive liked learned skimmers.
Baby foxes are just beginners,
They are just playful grinners.
Hyenas are always up for a fight,
You wait until you see them at night.
Ostriches are peckish birds,
You will never see them in herds.
Camels are humped creatures,
They may spit, but they're no screechers.
All of these mammals and birds
You will find in the zoo.

**Francesca Jarman (10)**
**South Wootton Junior School, King's Lynn**

# Vets

Barking and tweeting,
Screaming and shouting,
Bashing and crashing,
Miaowing and hissing . . .

Flying and crying,
De-fleaing and pouncing,
Paying and obeying,
Moaning and groaning,
Coughing and bleeding . . .

Feeding and eating
And that's not all . . .
Waiting and watching,
Calling and counting . . .
But they have to get well in the end!

**Evalyn Drake (8)**
**South Wootton Junior School, King's Lynn**


# At The Cinema

Popping and fading,
Munching and crunching,
Booing and hissing,
Chewing and kissing,
Chuckling and giggling,
Slurping and sniggering,
Of the children in the cinema.

Running and falling,
Creeping and crawling,
Kicking and crushing
Cans without a care.

**Carys Gill (8)**
**South Wootton Junior School, King's Lynn**

# Haiku - Seasons

*Spring*
Lively newborn lambs
Colourful blossom on trees
Sunny days begin

*Summer*
Fiery red sun beams
Twittering songs float from trees
Scorching golden sand

*Autumn*
Nut-nibblers scatter
Colourful, crisp, swirling leaves
Fiery-red sunset

*Winter*
Sparkling spiderwebs
Blanket of crunchy diamonds
Flickering fires.

**Kate Dewey (11)**
**South Wootton Junior School, King's Lynn**